screams

from childhood

Barbara Rogers

Barabara Press

Barabara Press
www.barabarapress.com

ISBN 0-971-9097-2-5
Library of Congress Control Number: 2004097958

Excerpt from "The Masculinization of Wealth" from *Moving Beyond
Words: Age, Rage, Sex, Power, Money, Muscles: Breaking the Boundaries of
Gender* by Gloria Steinem, Simon & Schuster, reprinted with the
author's permission. Copyright © 1994 by Gloria Steinem

**to Hannah and Marlene,
my enchanting granddaughters,
and to the children murdered in the Holocaust**

a hero child

Two dreams encouraged my work on this book. In the first dream I have a horrible, black, ugly-looking wound on my left upper arm. A little see-through pipe begins to grow out of this wound and turns into a tiny hand. Then another hand grows out of the other side of the wound, and above those tiny arms grows the tiny face of a child—called in the dream a hero child.

Through my work in therapy, a painful childhood wound became visible, was attended to, and a brave child grew out of this work—the child who always wanted to speak up but never could— and never dared to defend herself. My true Self and I accompany and support her in writing this book and telling about her ordeal.

For many years, my fear of speaking up about my parents' mistreatments and crimes paralyzed me—as if I was committing a crime if I told the truth about my childhood. In the second dream, I am in front of a tribunal in a big public hearing. I know that I have not committed a crime; but I am accused for my convictions.

My mother rises and declares that my convictions are wrong, impossible, and also dangerous. I speak up: "Be on my side—or leave." Infuriated and insulted, she marches out of the hall. People storm out of the assembly hall with her. Among them I recognize my sisters and other members of my family. At the end of my dream I am not on trial anymore. I am walking down a street by myself. I have won my freedom—in solitude.

As a German born in 1950, my life has been marked by the question of how the unspeakable crimes committed by Nazi Germany could have happened. True—political, historical, social, and religious factors all contributed to the rise of the fanatic, fascist regime. But—severe, strict, often violent and cruel child-rearing practices were also an important, and often overlooked, factor.

Human beings are not born evil but can be programmed to

act in evil ways, if mistreatment and cruelty are inflicted on innocent and powerless children. Aside from our spoken language, we teach our children a behavioral language that forms them deeply and has lasting consequences. I believe that inhuman child-raising methods created a volatile reservoir of repressed emotional energy, whose destructive power Hitler and his movement found easy to unleash.

My book and these "screams" are the result of a long search and a painful struggle. Aside from therapeutic writing on my own, I worked for many years with different therapists and different forms of therapy. I see myself as a searcher who has deeply explored her past and her unconscious, and who submits her report.

My personal journey led me to leave the family I grew up in, my first marriage, my country, my upper-class life, and the religion of my youth. Parts of my journey I have described in the essay "Facing a Wall of Silence" in the book *Second Generation Voices*, where I wrote, "I see my life as being in the service of overcoming silences, within me and around me."

With my book, I want to help overcome the silence about childhood suffering and its consequences, which a misused and misleading concept of forgiveness towards parents has imposed upon us. The most difficult process for me was to believe and embrace my abused, suffering inner child and to learn to be on her side in order to help her move past her fears and overwhelming feelings of powerlessness.

These "screams" were written over a period of twenty years. I see them as emotional paintings of the child's feelings and of the reality I could not be aware of and know as a child. I, the mature woman, have given the child my brain and my voice to express them. Like the pieces of a puzzle compose eventually a coherent picture, my childhood becomes manifest as each "scream" reveals moving insights about it. Through the "screams," the truth can come to light.

table of contents

chapter 1—a way out
walls   3
don't tell the truth   5
walled in   7
my anger is my lover   8
the screams provide the way out   10

chapter 2—no needs allowed
no needs allowed   13
if you do something for yourself   16

chapter 3—Hotto, tragic gift of life
Hotto   19
never again   20
Hotto's children   22
Hotto memories   23
leaving Hotto   26

chapter 4—creating connections:
    screams of freedom, joy and love
when I feel   31
resurrecting Barbara   32
two grandparents provide safety   33
on the island   35
Jan   37
my captain   40

chapter 5—lies
lies   45
virtue   47
the big black hole   49
mother church, house of stone   51

I

chapter 6—approval addict

approval addict   55
little circus horse   56
the starving lion and the lonely snail   57
the special child   58
competitive madness   60
haunted   62

chapter 7—the eldest

harbor   65
the fire   66
on the pedestal   68
harbor revisited   69
leading role   71

chapter 8—tyrant fear

Nikolaus   75
chaos   76
tin soldier   77
I won't let go   78
confirmation   80
life and death   82
the Jew in the family   83

chapter 9—in between

at the dinner table   87
the photo   89
broken heart—twisted heart   91
in between   92
how can I love?   94

chapter 10—battlefield child

battlefield child   97
the army of the believers   99
brainwashed   100
trapped   101
no place for me   102

chapter 11—extinguishing a woman

revisiting the Queen Mary—at the scene of the crime	105
three kinds of women	107
blindness and manipulation	109
father, unscrupulous	111

chapter 12—never on my side

the emperor	115
against me	116
thicket in the dark forest	118
telling the truth heals	120
would you have held me?	122
see—I told you so	124
one-way street to pity	125
fallen out of grace	126

chapter 13—seeking connection

beggar child	129
three hugs	130
without answer	131
it's all over	133
abyss	135
I thought you would be my friend	137

chapter 14—abandoned

your hand	141
the bride	142
the car accident	143
false guilt versus true guilt	145
not alone anymore	146
the betrayal of guilt	147

chapter 15—losing my mind

why do I have to believe so much?	151
the unnoticed injury	153
the manic-depressive see-saw	154
the judge who also prosecutes	156
requiem for an unlived life	158

chapter 16—worthless

swamp of worthlessness	163
shadows	164
a son is a god	165
worthless	166

chapter 17—who is my father?

what did you do in the war?	169
who is my father?	170
arrogance	172
betrayed	174
a man with charm	176
Ritzka	177
three monkeys	178

chapter 18—I wanted to be a writer

contradiction	181
the crime of having an imagination	182
women can't write	183

chapter 19—without parents

Hitler's children	187
lost values	188
control	189
merciless	190
accepting the truth	191
escaping	192
what I wish I had said	193

chapter 20—painful layers of silence

unbearable silence	197
painful layers of silence	198
incest—answered with silence	200
the curse of silence	202

chapter 21—hopeless

night and day	205
actions	206
the trap	208
lonely star	209
the bird and the wall	210

chapter 22—hatred—the banned feeling

    call it by its true name   213

    what the language of hatred reveals   214

    the language of love   216

chapter 23—a twisted concept of revenge

    dreams of justice   219

    mask of discipline   220

    sunday school   222

    a new journey   224

chapter 24—farewells

    leaving the fjord   227

    synagogue   228

    out of the fog   230

    hopeless hope   231

    the mountain or—changing perspective   232

    who am I?   234

    NO—my hidden guide through life   235

    black figure   237

    free   238

chapter 25—bringing forgiveness to the child who was never forgiven

    buried under a mountain of tar   241

    the land of unforgiveness   242

    we shed pain and hatred   243

    forgiveness—what does it mean?   244

    the land of forgiveness   246

chapter 26—walking together into life

    my feelings are like a universe   249

    the child—coming into my arms   250

    walking together into life   251

1
a way out

walls

written in Chicago, 1982

walls, nothing but walls—dark, impenetrable, threatening
they surround me—they have sapped my strength
they rise high in front of me, huge, steep, invincible
they stand between me and other people
between me and my children—me and my husband
between me and being alive
built of fear and pain
they separate me from freedom and being my Self
they consist of a long struggle with anxiety, only tamed by Valium
I have not taken this drug for the three months I've been
in therapy—thirty-two years old

a storm of unknown feelings overwhelms me
I have pneumonia and high fever
I also have my first dream in therapy
the first dream I can remember in my whole life

>I am cuddled with a blanket into a corner of my therapist's couch
>when three furious black figures enter his office
>my therapist gets up and argues with them
>I am surprised how angry
>my gentle, patient and kind therapist has become
>outside in the hallway I hear many, many children screaming
>I remove the blanket and put on my shoes
>with the hopeless feeling that I have to leave this room
>—where I feel safer and more secure than I ever felt in my life—
>to go back to these screaming children

alone at home the dream frightens me
anxiety, despair and loneliness crush me
only once a week can I see the doctor
with whom can I share this chaos inside of me?

I look for a pen and a piece of paper—and I write
it is the first time that I give a name to my feelings
that I try to put them into words
suddenly they become visible on the paper in front of me
but I don't understand what I am reading

the paper is patient and not afraid—it listens
I can entrust my thoughts to it—I can ask questions
why are there walls? who built them?
how can I tear them down? why is life such a burden?
how I wish I could walk with more ease and confidence
how tired am I of dragging my leaden legs

I have had glimpses of the other side of these walls—moments
when I felt alive—experienced colors, diversity, challenge
not this snarl of fear, pain and confusion
my desire to get to the other side is strong and wild
but the other side seems too distant—too far away
like another planet, another solar system—inaccessible to me

the doctor is not afraid of my feelings—can he help me?
it took so much courage to enter therapy—to say—*I need help*
I am the eldest of six children
I must support, hold and guide the people around me

once the doctor said to me—*can you not talk about yourself here*
because you don't want to be a problem for me?
the first tears in therapy rolled down my cheeks
—the source of a great stream—as I answered
no, I cannot be a problem—I have always tried to be perfect
the doctor turned around and handed me a box of Kleenex
with a little serious smile he said—*this is for all the perfect people*

that evening at home I was lying in the darkness of a room
I listened to music—he had touched me deep inside
I felt as if I was filled with a black, heavy, viscous mass
like sticky tar—the doctor enabled me to feel it
this day, this session gave me hope—I want to find a way out

don't tell the truth

my mother has called from Germany to inform me
that my father—sunk into depression at sixty-eight—
was admitted to a psychiatric hospital with paranoid thoughts

my mother forbids me to inform my brother
I tell my mother that my brother has to know
he has to find out the truth from his family—not through others
he will feel abandoned and betrayed when he has to wonder
why his own family remained silent
he might believe that the family blames him
and should he accuse himself—he might feel left out and isolated
—yet my mother is adamant that I remain silent

my brother and I have become friends since both of us
live far away from Germany
for the first time I feel close to someone in my family

my brother had a serious confrontation with our father recently
to free himself from his father's destructive control
I know that my brother has to know
I know that he is not responsible for my father's problems
I know that my father has been running away from himself
because he never dealt with his family past or war past
therapy is taboo where I come from

I cannot hand over my brother to silence and betrayal
the moment I hang up I call my brother—I tell him the truth
that day and during the following days
we have long conversations
as we try to come to terms with this news
he feels guilty—I try to convince him that he is not—
I am sure that my father's past has caught up with him

but I have done what my mother asked me not to do
I have contradicted her with my action
now I am in trouble
my anxiety has returned—has captured my body and mind
I also feel the responsibility for my brother
he has suffered greatly from my parents' authoritarian practices
my mother once revealed
that she was especially hard with this brother—her oldest son—
so that he would not turn out like her own brother
who was treated as the very special first-born son, too

I have acted against my mother's wishes
I have followed my conscience—I am so different from my mother
an abyss exists between us
I am passionate about being honest and open
I am against hiding the truth

yet my mother's thinking torments me
should my brother hurt himself—it would be my fault
because I told him the truth—I feel blamed and declared guilty

as the familiar anxiety keeps me from sleeping
I call a therapist I have met through friends
at first I say that I need to come
because I want to help my brother
but that does not get me anywhere

finally I manage to utter—*I need help*—but he has no time
I fight—*let me come when you have a cancellation*
I convince him—and my therapeutic journey begins

walled in

I grew up in a big house
surrounded by a high wall
an impressive staircase led up to the entrance door
framed by two big columns
up there I could overlook the huge garden and the swimming pool
—to people on the outside I was growing up in paradise

I did not know about life outside
I was not allowed to leave this walled-in world
except for visits to my grandparents, the island in the summer
or to go to school—I was seven or eight years old
when a boy from my class came to the big gate
he rang our doorbell and wanted to play with me
I went to the gate and opened it—but I had to send him away

fascinated by life outside of the big wall
I felt sad and lonely inside
I could not make sense of anything
my sorrow and pain were shoved away
you have everything—a swimming pool—rich parents
you live in a big beautiful house with a big beautiful garden
how dare you complain—what is your problem?

I did not feel I had everything—only rarely
could I spend time with my parents
I lived far away from them
on the third floor, in a different world from theirs
where nannies took care of me

my anger is my lover

my anger is my lover—my anger knows the truth
my anger remembered the incest that plunged
the sixteen-year-old into a morass of confusion, anxiety, despair

I had to hide the truth from myself because the small child
had felt safe with a father who never beat her
she could not bear the truth
her father meant closeness, security, survival and joy of life to her

when my anger started to tell me about the incest
this child inside made the anger go away again and again
this young girl cried for weeks in therapy—*my father loves me*
my father would never do this to me
terrified she fought the truth—she believed
that she never could survive the loss
of the image of a loving father

I was not angry as a child—I was not the family rebel
on the contrary—I was the family showpiece

but the anger survived like a submarine in the depths
it waited until it was safe to surface

when it trusted me and my work in therapy and was sure that
—confronted with the truth—I would not be afraid anymore
or believe I must be crazy to remember something so awful
my anger articulated clearly—*your father was irresponsible*
he abused you unimaginably—he committed the crime of incest
and, I am sure, other crimes you don't know about
what did he do in the war?
he was capable of lying to everyone
he continued his life as if nothing had happened

but the child who trusted and loved her father needs time
to mourn the loss of her idol—every therapy session helps her
with time my anger is liberated to be a seeker of truth
and becomes my engaged mentor

after I listen to her and comfort her patiently
the child can let go of her illusions
and evolves as a treasured part of my aliveness and love of life
now I can face the truth about the incest and other child abuse

banned from my inner world and emotional repertoire
my anger appeared at first like a dark and monstrous giant
who caused overwhelming fear
among other identities who lived inside of me
—the ones who tried to please and clung to illusions—
they had been running the human being named Barbara
they were terrified to recognize reality

slowly my anger reveals the truth until I can live with the facts
it helps me confront old pain inside—it welcomes my true Self

my anger becomes my lover who wears colorful, exotic clothes
who wants me to be true to my Self and speak my truth
this lover gives me the strength to say *no* and create boundaries

this lover teaches me that I never was bad or wrong
never an evil or worthless child—but informs me of the truth
that the people into whose care the child's life was entrusted
hurt me through evil attitudes and actions
through inhuman methods of treating children

my lover supports me to dare to venture into life
and to walk proudly and freely
my lover encourages me to make my dreams come true

secretly and quietly, behind the scenes, never in loud ways
this lover has guided my life most amazingly

the screams provide the way out

I did not want to know about the hell of fear and pain
the nightmares of loneliness and confusion
inside me

unconscious truth continued its work of destruction
because I was not supposed to voice my screams

hidden away like a shameful original sin
they had to remain underground deep inside
horrors of childhood
passed on from generation to generation

as I studied the dark night of my childhood
I have learned to see truthfully

I have come to realize that my screams are not crimes
but most precious messengers of a buried past

the screams reveal the emotional reality of my childhood
they show me the truth of the powerless child
they reveal her total dependency
they paint, with words and feelings, the child's ordeal

the screams become my truth
provided by life and nature to save a soul

voicing my screams is my key to freedom and life
voicing the screams that could never live
and were never heard
becomes my way out

2
no needs allowed

"In the German ideal of upbringing, whatever was creative was killed. If it danced out of line and did something that did not reflect the authoritarian father or mother, it got thrashed." Furthermore, *"in Germany, when a child of nine months still wets its pants, it is a catastrophe. And mothers among themselves were proud [if they could say] 'Ja, my child is already clean.' That was such a tradition. One should not undervalue these small things. These little mosaic stones, I find, were already there and really paved the way for something like Hitler."—Karma Rauhut*

Alison Owings, *Frauen: German Women Recall the Third Reich*

no needs allowed

needs were wrong—forbidden early on
the baby's hunger—controlled by the clock
allowed only every four hours—and not at night

to hold or feed a crying child at night or outside of schedule
was considered spoiling the child and raising a willful monster

the innocent baby's screams were ignored
with inconceivable inhumanity
as the whims of a spoiled brat that had to be tamed

potty trained—through physical violence—by the age of one
the baby learned to deliver those unspeakable things
in the right place at the desired time
the child sat for endless times on a potty
tied to the bars of the playpen

thirst was declared bad for children
I could not ask for something to drink
something to drink was only granted at certain meals
and it was not enough

to want food between meals was also a crime
secret excursions into the pantry brought severe punishment
if they were discovered

my expressions of love were unwanted—my mother dismissed
the need for tenderness and closeness as "monkey love"

not allowed to leave my parents' world
ballet lessons labeled as—*too affected and effeminate*
my need for friendship—cut off until I was ten years old

then I could spend time with other children
but could not join the girl scouts because
others always want something from us

my body's need to develop freely and independently was blocked
the child had to endure frightening, humiliating enemas
and icy showers
the teenager was gynecologically examined
then my mother and the pediatrician decided
something was wrong with me—so I had to rinse my vagina
with purple water—sitting in a plastic bowl—to start
my menstruation that was—"too slow" and "too late" to show up

my need to love my body—exorcised
my mother lifted my blanket when I was a teenager to check
that my hands did not touch that disgusting, dirty part of my body

my need and right for my sexual awakening—turned
into a nightmare of guilt and shame
my need for love—perverted to incest

feelings, thoughts, questions coming from a child
were regarded as stupid and worthless
the need to express them—banned

my own voice—silenced
eradicated by intolerance and dictatorial censorship
my need for self-expression—extinguished
by derision and condescension

my need for honesty, openness and truth—crashed
into walls of lies and silence—was deeply betrayed
and became twisted into telling others what they wanted to hear

my deep need for integrity became stunted
as I was turned into an obedient follower—a smiling pretender
—a polite "yes-man"—who did not dare
to think freely or speak her mind truthfully

my need for recognition and respect—perverted
into the coercion of having to shine
having to impress others with unimportant things
while love, creativity and the blossoming of my true Self
were contemptuously rejected

my need for justice—suppressed by a system
where the law was on my parents' side—and always against me
I had no witness—no advocate on my side

my need to feel safe—perverted into letting others hurt me
resigned itself to accepting cruelty as—my problem
as the result of—my evilness—my guilt

my need for mercy and compassion—extinguished
under burdens of blame and punishment
while my parents demanded—and were granted—
unconditional forgiveness and understanding

the child—who wandered in a maze without exit—
wanted to know—*what did you do in the war, father?*
but the need to ask questions was silenced too

my need for truth—portrayed as childish and presumptuous
my need to experience and speak my truth——numbed
by judgments, punishments and beatings—later by tranquilizers

———————————

needs—fought and battled from the very beginning
became unrecognizable demons that lurked in the dark
filling my body with shame and fear when they tried to surface

for you whose needs were not honored
I give you my screams from childhood

if you do something for yourself

I have written to one of my sisters that I have entered therapy
she responds with a letter where I stumble over the sentence
that doing therapy is *"elitist and anti-social"*

as I read these words I am overwhelmed by anxiety
it won't go away and is so strong that I dare to call my therapist

my anxiety disappears the moment he says
your family is against you when you do something for yourself

I find it utterly unimaginable—there are places in this world
where I am not judged as selfish and wrong
      if I want to get off drugs
      try to communicate with my soul
      try to change the fear that rules me
      try to help the agony of my mind
      if I long to claim my voice and my life

a powerful truth reaches me
there are human beings who live differently from my family
they see our true Selves as being entrusted to us
to be cherished, nurtured and unfolded
to let them live and shine

they regard our true Self as a precious gift that life entrusts to us
they consider caring for it
as our life's essential responsibility and task

I hang up the telephone stunned and peaceful
my life is changed forever

3
Hotto, tragic gift of life

Hotto

written in 2001

I am on the little train going to the harbor of the island
where I used to spend my childhood summers
I am forty-one years old
for a few days I have visited my childhood nanny
who has lived on this island for many years
she came into my life when I was one year old—she left
when I was seven years old—for six years she lived with me

my visit is over and I am leaving the island
I stand on a little platform outside of the train compartment
while the train chugs to the harbor it passes by her house
as I look over I realize that Hotto is standing outside of her home
with her husband and son at her side
they are looking for me—waving at me—saying goodbye
I am waving too—I am so glad to see them one more time

suddenly—from the bottom of my soul
from an unknown depth of my being
emerges a tremendous scream—makes its way out into the world
surprising and shocking me
"HOTTO"—I scream as loud as I can—*"HOTTO"*

the child with all her love and longing and hidden pain
shows me the essential importance of a life-saving relationship
and its tragic loss for my life

remembering my Hotto scream on the train
—this precious moment of communication with my soul—
and writing it down today—another ten years later
my tears return while I write her name—HOTTO
I am still mourning her loss

never again

for years I suffered when I traveled
always right before or on the day of my trip I would get ill
and often during my trip too

the days before I had to leave—filled
with unbearable tension and restlessness
with apprehension and fears about leaving and going away
I became anxious, agitated, easily irritated, even desperate
it was terribly hard for me to separate from people or places

I am about to go on my first trip since I have entered therapy
I arrive for my last session the day before I leave
full of anxiety all I can say is—*I feel horrible—I am filled with fear*
        I feel as if I have lost my center
my therapist says—*your father used to travel a lot*
        it was hard for you when he went away
        this is how you felt as a child
I answer—*but I had my own life later as a teenager*
        then my father was not important to me anymore
the doctor responds—*your father meant life to you*

as I hear these words I burst into tears
I cry for a long time as I have never cried in my life
as I walk out of his office I realize that my center is back

on the first night of the trip that follows
I have a nightmare which awakens me terror-stricken
        in the kitchen of the house where I last lived in Germany
        I have put my mother in a garbage bag—then a garbage press
        at the end of the dream I sit on my kitchen bench
        and look at this garbage bag in front of me that contains
        my compressed mother—and I don't know what to do with it

the first dream I ever had about my mother fills me with horror

during this trip I get very ill with a severe ear infection
my brain is obsessed with fear and worrying
will I make it back in time for my next session?

when I finally return I am so angry and upset that I cannot talk
my therapist says—*this is how a child feels when it is left behind*
how did your children react when you went away?

I remember how often my children cried when I returned
even after just a few hours—and the baby-sitter would say—
they were fine until now
I remember with painful regret and rage those three days
when my oldest son had to stay in a hospital in Germany
he was only two years old—I was not allowed to visit him
—when he saw me again he turned away from me

here on the doctor's couch, all these years later
I understand my son's reaction
as I feel the child's pain over devastating separations

———————

in my therapy and in my life
every separation, every loss of a relationship
brought up Hotto's leaving with excruciating pain
as a severe trauma of my childhood

the child is still waiting for Hotto—full of disbelief
silently, horrified and petrified
her eyes are still watching Hotto leave and disappear
the grownup woman I am becoming can hold this girl
understand her and bear her screams

———————

to avoid being hurt like this again the child made two vows
—never again would she let anyone be close to her
—and never again would she trust the feeling of love

Hotto's children

written in 1987

back in Germany I live again in my hometown
minutes away from my parents—surrounded by relationships
which have made me very unhappy for a long time

when I can make the decision to move away I dream
>   that I come up the stairs in the big house where I grew up
>   with my parents and nannies and brothers and sisters
>   until I got married
>   when I reach the second floor I go to Hotto's room
>   I had not remembered what her room looks like
>   but this dream shows it to me and I recognize it clearly
>
>   as I enter the room I see Hotto's wooden, antique bed
>   I see Hotto standing next to the bed
>   I ask her—*Hotto, where are the children?*
>   Hotto points to the bed—where I discover two children
>
>   one of them I know really well as if I have known her all my life
>   she is the good Barbara who did everything well and right
>   she was the way everyone wanted her to be
>
>   but the other child next to her
>   is a child I have never ever looked at or noticed
>   she is the alive—real—Barbara
>   with wishes, feelings, needs, thoughts and dreams of her own
>   she reaches out for me and hugs me
>   passionately, fervently, for a long time
>   profound feelings of gratitude and love emanate from her

I wake up deeply moved

Hotto memories

during my visit to the island
Hotto shows me a black and white photo of my sister and me
we are about two and three years old
I am moved—how enchanting we look
but stunned to see us wearing beautiful dresses
I remember how my mother opposed anything pretty
as frivolous, superfluous, unnecessary clothing
Hotto tells me that she begged my mother for months
to give her money to buy fabric for these dresses
which Hotto herself sewed for us

———————————

Hotto tells me how we met—your parents at that time
lived on the upper floor of your grandparents' house
my room was a small garret in a huge, dark, unfinished attic
if I had not been so afraid of the dark
I would have run away that first night

I was inspected most carefully
right away during the first hours I was supposed to feed you
three adults—your mother, father
and the nurse who took care of your newborn sister
were watching me spellbound
you beamed at me—you accepted me spontaneously
you made the difference—and I stayed

then you could not walk by yourself
you did that for the first time on my birthday in June
which is why I remember it so clearly

———————————

Hotto's father worked in a coal mine
they lived on the other side of town

when Hotto went home to her parents on her weekend off
she described to them what the rich family where she was living
would eat for their meals and she told her parents
we eat better than they do

———————————

born at yearly intervals we three sisters shared a bedroom
where we were shoved away to bed always much too early

my sister remembers with breathtaking clarity
horrible scenes from our childhood
she recalls how we were lying in the dark
not allowed to use light, to read or to talk
I told stories to ease our loneliness—but if Hotto would hear it
she would come in to beat all three of us with a dress hanger

my sister recounts—*Hotto would always beat you first*
the youngest sister next—and then she would come to me
*but I would plead with her—**please, please, Hotto, DON'T!***
and then Hotto would hit me only once

you would be lying there in the dark—sobbing
you always had such a tendency to make a fuss about things
this last remark about me my sister says with contempt

———————————

Hotto tells me how she left—*for a long time*
I had been playing with the thought of becoming a midwife
but the tuition was a lot of money for my parents and me
finally the moment was there—I gave notice a whole year ahead
your father made my life difficult from then on
he only talked with me officially and reproached me
saying I acted irresponsibly towards the five of you

*maybe he was right—until then you actually were **my** children*
but I also wanted to make my dreams come true

you and your brothers and sisters never seemed changed to me

but you never talked to me about anything anymore
—whereas before I got to know everything

_____

when I was ten years old
Hotto came back to stay with us again for another two years
to help when my youngest brother was born
years later—I was a mother by then but not yet in therapy—
she told me about her return which I had forgotten
she said—*when I came back you were not "my" child anymore*
I answered spontaneously
maybe I was angry at you for leaving me

_____

the summer after I have started therapy
I visit my parents on the island
I call Hotto whom I have not seen in years
therapy has brought up memories of her

while I talk to Hotto on the phone I notice the expression
on my mother's face across from me
bitter, insulted, angry—her strong resentment
that I make this phone call to reach out to Hotto fills the room
her expression says, without words—*how can you do this to me*
Hotto hears my voice and says with warmth
what is the matter, Barbara? you sound sad

in this moment I grasp
the treacherous entanglement of the relationships
between me—my mother—Hotto—and my father
where jealousy and resentment—bitterness and possessiveness
sided the rectangle that, as a child, I considered love

leaving Hotto

written in 2001

a stunning dream awakens me

in the dream I am with a child who looks just as I looked as a child
with the same dark hair and pageboy
she and I have been out on an adventure and have come home
before the child goes to bed
I have asked her to help me put something together for a project
I am waiting for her in a computer room
stairs lead into this unusual room at first onto a spacious platform
then a scary part drops down steeply
into a rectangular, breathtakingly deep hole—down there
the parts of a computer have to be put into their right places

as I look down I realize
I cannot send the child into this frightful abyss
I myself have to go down there to put those parts in
as I stand on the upper platform and wait for the child
it eventually becomes obvious
that the door remains closed—she is not coming
so I open the door and leave the room—outside I see Hotto
she tells me that the child cannot come to join me
because she has to go to bed and sleep
I respond that I had agreed with the child
that she would bring me those parts that we need
and help me before she sleeps

Hotto and I stand at the open door
we confront each other with our eyes and wills
what matters is not what the child does
but to whom she belongs—who has power over her

it is the key moment of my dream

Hotto wants the child to sleep—I want her to come alive
the child has obeyed Hotto and gone away
she is standing at the end of a long hallway, far away from me

I win the argument in the dream with my eyes
through the way I look at Hotto
I win with my words and the tone of my voice
I win through endurance and persistence
I claim the child from Hotto
she becomes my child and she comes to me
from now on, we work together

as I wake up I remember above all
how this child looks at me at the end of the dream
as she brings those parts to me
her unforgettable look says—*am I finally your child?*
are you now truly there for me? do I truly belong to you?
the expression on her face says she is ready to be with me
it speaks of serious, excited anticipation

this dream is followed by the most difficult months of therapy
at the mercy of overwhelming anxiety I hardly sleep
night after night I write—week after week I work hard in therapy
I enter a long dark night of the soul—clinically called a depression
as the child reveals how she was dangerously attacked
as a very small child by her own mother

for several days I fear that I am going crazy as the child reveals
how she was nearly killed as a small child by her own mother
I must experience her earliest, most devastating trauma
and its frightening consequences for my mind
to recognize and overcome them emotionally

my voice, my screams, were silenced with brutal force
as something was shoved deep down my throat
I was in mortal danger—pushed into deadly fear
my mother tries to kill me
how could the child ever come to terms with that reality?

there is a recurring feeling of a strong pain that I know all too well
it climbs several times up and down and up and down
from inside my chest all the way up to my throat
once in a while it returns—my body remembers

my massage therapist's touch has calmed me for years
on her table I have shed tears and shared emotional wounds
on her table the child dares to communicate her greatest trauma

one day during the dark night of the soul panic overwhelms me
as her hands move along my body
and I am persecuted by the obsessive thought
I am in mortal danger—she is going to kill me
afraid to tell my massage therapist what races through my head
I remain silent, believing full of anxiety that she will say I am crazy
I stumble out of her office—and for the first time in years
I take a tranquilizer to calm my body trembling from fear

the following week I can share my experience with her
she responds—*it happens often*
even when I touch people for the first time
that traumatic childhood memories return
I ask her—*what do people do if they are not in therapy?*
they take drugs—is her answer
luckily I am in therapy and my adult mind
—with the help of my therapists and my closest friend—
helps the child survive the unimaginable, unendurable truth
my mother silenced me by attacking me
my mother almost killed me

during the following weeks I struggle and cough while I talk
as my suffocated voice returns

I have reached the terrified child
who was frozen in deadly fear for fifty years
because her life was threatened by her own mother

now I begin to speak with my own voice—I am reborn

4
creating connections:
screams of freedom, joy and love

when I feel

when I
feel
I can be
my Self

when I feel
I can be me
I
Barbara

when I feel
I am

when I feel
I am my Self
I can be my Self
I know that I am alive

when I feel
life is streaming through me
its light shines on my soul
and I connect with life and people around me

when I feel
I am me
I
Barbara

resurrecting Barbara

I have been in therapy for eighteen months
when I have to leave Chicago, the beloved, treasured world
where I have come to enjoy my life
have become engaged in life
active as a chamber musician and in my children's school
taking a college class
making real friends for the first time in my life

my first husband has pushed through what he has longed for
but what I dread—our return to Germany

at the end of those first eighteen months of therapy I dream that
> **I am sitting on the doctor's couch**
> **in front of me is a grave that has been opened**
> **I see a body in there—wrapped with white bandages**
> **it looks like a mummy**
>
> **sobbing and crying**
> **overwhelmed by compassion and with the utmost tenderness**
> **I sink into the grave**
> **to embrace and hold**
> **the corpse that was buried in that grave**

Barbara was buried—for too many years—
until I uncovered her grave with the doctor's help

I have resurrected a Barbara
that no one wanted to exist
the alive Barbara with feelings, thoughts, needs
dreams and wishes
of her own

two grandparents provide safety

soon after I left my first marriage I dreamt that
> I had escaped
> a tightly secured and fiercely guarded fortress
> surrounded by huge walls and barbed wire
> protected by scary, aggressive dogs
> as I got away from that frightening place
> my children were with me
> I took us into safety
> by bringing them to the two grandparents I loved
> —my mother's father and my father's mother—

---

visits to our paternal grandmother were childhood highlights
we children fought fiercely over our turns

I loved her old-fashioned apartment that I still can see and smell
she had a musical bird in a golden cage
I enjoyed hearing it sing—and remember the melody it whistled

my grandmother had time and patience
she loved company
I was allowed to watch TV and eat chocolate with her
we also played games together or talked
the most wonderful thing—to be allowed to stay for dinner
I recall the silver knife holders that decorated her elegant table
I can taste the delicious dark bread and hard-boiled eggs
I loved the nicely prepared and tasty food I was served
I felt special and welcome
I spent peaceful times with her—away from chaos and noise

once I asked her what her names were
they seemed so old fashioned to me
that I laughed, learned them and know them to this day
Friederike, Therese, Emma, Wilhelmine
and Irma—the name we shared

I remember my maternal grandfather as a kind and gentle man
he had time for me—took me seriously
he enjoyed my visits
when I was a teenager we had real conversations
and I played the piano for him
he did not show me off but listened
delighted at my progress
amazed that I adored Bach

I can see the chair where he used to sit
often with a brown fuzzy blanket over his thin legs
his hands, bent by age, were lying in his lap
he could not play the piano anymore

I have a note from my grandfather, which I treasure
he wrote it to my mother while I visited England as a teenager
> your daughter's letters from England are written
> in the style of the grand ladies of the eighteenth century
> she is a talented writer
it brings a smile to my face when I read it

I felt very close to these two grandparents
I cannot remember them ever being angry or impatient with me

on the island

the island meant paradise—the paradise of summer
the island brought the light of freedom and connection

my life became guided by the longing and search
to bring the island's magic back—to make it come true for my life

I spent every summer on the island with my family
my grandfather bought the house as a summer retreat
the island seemed to change everyone—to bring out
different identities—a magical world transformed my parents
into freer, less burdened beings who imposed few rules

life became much more uncomplicated—less isolated
we seemed to live more like other families

free to do whatever I wanted, I had power over my life
—it was the greatest feeling—
I remember two rules—I had to be at home in time for meals
and when my father wanted a family excursion with the boat
we had to come along—but the rest of my time
I could spend however and wherever I wanted to

the island gave me the chance to be alone
how much time did I spend on the island by myself
there I could get away from the unbearable unrest in the house
from noise—tension—commands—orders—expectations

I loved books—and sometimes I read in my father's room
filled with memories he had collected all over the world
there I would listen to Chopin and read my favorite love novel

how I loved to come to the top of the dunes
where I could look down to the beach and sit for hours

to read—and to watch and listen to the sea that I adored
as a teenager I had my own little room at the end of the house
right by the stable—I got up early in the morning
saddled my mother's horse and rode to the beach
where I galloped and felt free

I loved the boat, which my mother avoided
I enjoyed sleeping and traveling on the boat
I remember the smell of diesel—the dampness of the sheets
I have an alive, warm inner picture of the boat
and of the room of my own on the island

on the island I could work
digging up weeds between bricks and sweeping the street
I earned a little money and could buy something I wanted
I felt power
as a teenager I had saved enough money
for half of my dream bike—my parents added the other half
I bought the light blue painted beauty
I was its proud owner and rode it everywhere

the island meant having neighbors
I was free to meet and play with other children
across the street lived Jan with his parents
their summer guests were lots of boys
in the evening I played soccer with them—on the meadow
behind our house—the laundry posts became our goals
I spent time at the beach with other children
participated in games

life was incomparably different on the island
from in the industrial town where we spent the rest of the year
surrounded and visited by lots of people
—mostly people who seemed to be related to us—
I felt isolated and separated there from the world around me
lonely and abandoned within my own and extended family

I always felt like a stranger in my family

Jan

Jan wanted to be a singer
he studied singing in a big city
and returned to his home, the island, for the summer
he taught tennis and was a lifeguard at the beach
my father was a passionate tennis player and loved sports
so I had to take tennis lessons—Jan became my teacher

I was allowed to go over to his home to practice the piano
I was always welcome—I could just enter the house to play
sometimes Jan listened or even made music with me
I accompanied him while he sang songs
I loved to hear him sing
his company made me deeply happy

I see his gentle alive face with a warm and joyful expression
his warm, blue eyes shining at me with a twinkle
I never experienced him angry or cold

I was twelve when we started to write letters during the time
when we were away from the island
how I treasured those letters—this relationship
he was fourteen years older—I was thrilled by his interest in me

I remember standing next to him on my father's boat
in a wild storm—I felt safe and confident next to him
as wave after wave hit the boat and us
until it was decided that we had to turn around and go back

indescribable joy—the joy of being with Jan—next to Jan
the joy of making music with Jan
of receiving letters from Jan—of writing to him
the joy of meeting him, secretly, at the beach at sunset
the joy of walking with him through the dunes

pushing our bicycles—while our hands are touching and holding
the joy of riding my bike—and of suddenly
feeling his arm around me
the joy of having him by my side

the joy when one day during a tennis lesson
we heard a dog cry in the distance—and I said
listen, it is your dog
we looked for him in the dunes and found him
caught in a trap—and Jan freed him

the joy of our eyes meeting when I arrived at the beach
where the light and glory of summer
were dancing and sparkling on the water
and I looked forward to him joining me in the water
where we enjoyed playfully each other's company
or jumped high waves in the stormy sea

the joy of our eyes meeting
when he left his home across from ours
in the evening on his bike
I would always find a way to join him
so that no one knew or noticed where I was going
because I had to escape brothers or sisters
who wanted to come along for a ride

the joy of the very first kiss I received when I was fourteen
the joy of finally being embraced by another human being
the joy of my company being enjoyed and treasured
the joy of doing so many things with him
the joy of being recognized for who I was
the joy of heavenly moments we had together

on the last evening
during that unforgettable summer when he kissed me
I remember sitting on his lap and stroking my hands
through his dark blond hair, over and over again
looking at him, overflowing with love and joy, delighted to be alive

the joy of having a nickname—Herzchen—my little heart
the joy of those little notes which he would hide after that summer
in the envelope's casing—so that my mother would not find them
notes where he wrote loving words—and my nickname
the joy of reading them over and over again
the joy of Jan

I know that I would not be who I am
without his powerful presence in my life

thirty years later I met a man who loves and treasures me
the memories of Jan and the island returned overwhelmingly
in the beginning of our relationship

how much he reminded me of my time with Jan

but this time
I was determined to get to the other side of the wall
where no one could ever again
take the joy of love away from me

my captain

when I met you I was forty-five years old
I had left all ties behind—was not dating
not interested in men anymore

I had set up my tripod and camera in a jazz club
you sat down in front of me—and turned around to talk to me
I can still hear your wonderful warm laugh
that I heard then for the first time—the laugh which I so love
I remember what we talked about

when I gathered my things on the little table in front of me
I found your card—I took it home—the image of the airplane
taking off against a sunset sky had touched me—
I thought about it for three days
my body and soul spoke clearly—they longed
for closeness and embraces—so I called you—and we met

I see you across the table where we had dinner
—with your black leather jacket
—with your sincere way of being and talking
that night I dreamt that my car went up high
—a terrifyingly steep mountain—only to be stuck way up
in a very dangerous and scary situation
that turned out to be terribly true
as I fell in love passionately, it brought up a buried past
that had shaped my fears of love and life

through great turmoil and hard emotional work
you stuck with me—remained at my side—never gave up on me
you always believed in me—you helped me claim my life
you encouraged me to face the incest and travel to the ship
you wanted me to become liberated and empowered
you touched my soul deeply—you became a true companion

you encouraged me to leave a therapeutic dead-end street
to entrust myself to different forms of therapy—and to my Self

love connected us from the beginning
love guided us out of deep valleys
love let us heal the hurt accumulated in both of us

you gave me the gift of coming alive sexually—but
that brought back the incest memory—and dark times for me
we both struggled—without your support my healing
and this journey—would not have been possible
the memories I have with you are indescribable
so beautiful and unforgettable
even painful moments and difficult times
only deepened our love, strengthened our walk together
our understanding of and compassion for each other
no matter what happened
your arms always welcomed and embraced me

how loved I felt our first night when my body could not respond
but you held me all night in your arms anyway
to tell me over and over again how you loved my brain
how treasured I felt—what a gift that was

how loved I felt when your arms just opened and held me
when we saw each other again
after I had broken off our relationship for awhile
how treasured and loved I felt when you told me
that you felt you were making love to me—by talking to me
we had been laying naked on your bed together for hours
on a warm summer day—I could not make love that day

how loved I felt in your arms
when I told you about my car accident—you listened
and expressed warm compassion for this tragic mark on my life
how supported I felt when you held and comforted me
spoke all the right words as I, sobbing and upset, remembered
—while we were making love—

remembered with great pain and shame
that my body had been capable of orgasm during incest

how alive and loved I felt during your first visit to my house
you gave me power over what we would do together that day
every time when I wondered what I would like us to do together
I smiled—I played Chopin's etude in A flat Major for you
then asked you to read what I had written about the Holocaust
thinking—*if he does not like how I think—he will be gone soon*
but you stayed and let me take you out for dinner
it was a wonderful day—from that very beginning
we have shared the dreams we dreamt during the night

you were patient and understanding with a woman
who was afraid to open her soul and her body—how alive
and loved I felt when my body and soul began to trust you
when making love became an exciting and passionate adventure
how I love your voice—especially when you sing
I feel alive when we dance and sing together
when I can share my Self with you
when we talk, when we make love
when we write and create and share our thoughts and journeys
when we work together—or side by side
when I perform a karate kata with you
when we go into the world
and bring back to each other our discoveries and adventures

you welcome my creativity, my spirit and true Self
your love is my home—your integrity a solid ground to walk on
your trust provides support and confidence
your encouragement and patience grant me strength
your honesty and sincerity build time and again
a moving bridge to me—that empowers me to be truthful

at your side
I left the darkness of guilt and blame, lies and hypocrisy behind
how I treasure your honesty and openness

5
lies

lies

she says—*I mean well*—and
beats
her child

her eyes speak a different language—of hate and bitterness
misery and pain—despair and revenge

the mother says—*I mean well*
but pain penetrates the body of the girl—then the soul
she cries out

I mean well—her mother repeats
the girl screams—*then why are you hurting me?*
I love you

you don't do what is my will—replies the mother
this is why I have to beat you

the girl cries—*I cannot always do what is your will*
sometimes I have to go my own way
I have a will, too
I have my own thoughts

the mother beats her daughter more forcefully, even harder
she screams—*I cannot bear that you have your own thoughts*
and you may not have a will of your own

you are a bad, evil, sinful girl if you have a will of your own
I will beat you until you admit that you are bad
until you admit that I am right

don't cry! don't scream! pull yourself together!
bear the pain! be quiet! once and for all!

you may only be the way I want you to be!

here—I rule!
here—my word is the law!
here—my power and my will are the law!

you
were bad
you
did not do—what I want you to do
you
did not think—how I want you to think
you
were not the way—I want you to be

this is your punishment—you deserve it

if you scream I will beat you even more
even longer and harder

say that you are bad
say that you will never do this again

the girl is laying on the ground
she sobs quietly and says—*please, mother, please, end it*
I am bad
I will never do this again
I am bad
forgive me

the mountain of hate from inside her mother
—the truth that the girl could read in her mother's eyes—
moves into the soul of the little girl

she has encountered the language of hatred

now she hates too—her mother
and she begins to hate—herself

virtue

written in Chicago, summer of 1986

lies are my gown
some call its fabric virtue
it covers me so that I can please—can please you, mother
in dresses of virtue I must hide my Self

how do I dress myself?
not the way I like—not the way I am
but so that I may read acceptance and admiration in your eyes

the truth is a simple gown—it would be my very own
woven of my very own fabric—my feelings, thoughts and needs
woven of honesty and openness
but you don't like it
you and my father—and so many others
cannot bear its sight
do not wish me to wear it

my truth is potent—filled with questions, curiosity, convictions
with my own ideas and wishes
with an endless search for joy, tenderness and love
but only if I disguise my truth in lies will you praise me
and can I please you

so I clothe my rage in complaisance
        my questions in humility
                my rebellion in silent withdrawal
                        my revenge in being useful
                                my curiosity in meaningless chatter
                        my sadness in cheerful calmness
                my joy in indifference
        my longing for justice in servility
thus my gown of lies is admired as virtue

I cannot dress myself anymore in the virtue of lies
the truth is burning within me

I put on its strict and simple suit
I carry its glowing fire
I want to let shine the flame of my longing for truth

the big black hole

little girl, so happy
the sun touches your body—the wind plays with your hair
you are skipping—excited to be alive
but your mother's voice says
don't skip!—skipping is wrong and bad! good girls don't skip!
little girl—your happiness turns into guilt

little girl, your sister has taken your doll—you are angry
your mother's voice says—*don't be angry! be nice and forgiving!*
good girls are never angry! good girls never fight!
little girl—your anger turns to guilt

little girl, you have played soccer with the boys
you are full of energy and life—but your mother complains
how disgusting you look! good girls look nice and orderly
she straightens out your long hair until you scream
little girl—your joy of life turns into pain

little girl, you came home from school
proud of your accomplishments—you want to share them
but your mother is waiting for you—hidden behind the door
all of a sudden she appears—and starts hitting you with a whip
little girl—your love of learning turns into fear

little girl, you have been injured and the cut at your wrist bleeds
you are terrified that your mother might find out—and punish you
how relieved you are when your father takes care of your wound
little girl—tragically you have to put all your trust
into a manipulative, dangerous father

little girl, you were hungry and took some food
you were thirsty and tried to drink—and also to cover your crimes
your mother's voice screams—*I told you—never steal food*

never lie! you need to be punished very hard! you are a bad girl!
little girl—hunger and thirst turn into guilt

little girl, you recognize that your mother does not tell the truth
your mother responds—*so what?*
I have simply lied—that's just the way it is
little girl, your soul screams—*who punishes you for lying, mother?*
you get away with everything—grown up and stronger than I am
little girl—you must give up your integrity

little girl, your truth is twisted into a lie
your rage over the injustice of your humiliating ordeal
overwhelms you—the world around you turns black

little girl, you want to tell your mother—*don't you see*
you teach me to act nice when I am angry
you teach me to act happy when I am sad
you teach me to be serious when I am happy
you teach me to lie—I am scared to death to tell the truth
little girl—your feelings and needs become an anxious jumble
they cannot guide your well-being, your health, your life anymore

little girl—you want to say your own thoughts—but your mother
warns you—*don't you dare have other thoughts than mine!*
God sees all your thoughts and all you do! always obey!
you go to hell if your thoughts are wrong and bad!
little girl—your mother's beliefs replace your identity

little girl, with so much pain, drowning in loneliness
your mother's voice demands—*pull yourself together*
you have no pain or suffering in your life—you have it all
your father can recognize the sadness in your eyes—but mocks
your sorrow—*only weaklings cry—be my brave little girl!*
little girl—your inside becomes a big black hole
that draws in nothing but guilt and anxiety

later—without your own feelings and thoughts—
your life is a hopeless struggle against this black void inside

mother church, house of stone

written in Germany, 1986

church—house of stone—beautiful to look at
but how cold to my touch

lifeless splendor—petrified beauty
built for exalted adoration and devoted submission
to a superior being I can't see
whom I don't know
malleable according to any arbitrary human belief

church—life and truth
replaced by dogmas and empty rules of morality
salvation depending on conditions—on the right belief
on the perfect and only true connection with the Higher Being

church—uncaring intolerance
authorized by a higher power

whatever is projected onto a Higher Being
reveals only what followers need to believe in

church—the powerless "down here"
dependent—upon a Higher Being "up there"
—far away and removed, inaccessible, unknowable—
how powerless is the child against the beliefs of Almighty Parents

church—a vital relationship—cast into stone and beliefs

church—when I touch you I freeze
and life fades from me like, mother, when I try to embrace you

church—house of stone
where I am suffocated by beliefs and hypocrisy

51

in church—I hear souls
filled by the screams of hurt children's pain
who yearn to be delivered and find salvation

church—exploits
the accumulated loads of guilt and loneliness in the child
and uses it to create a flourishing business

church—glorious facades—regulated relationships
where appearances replace reality
where questioning and free thinking are unwanted

church—silent place where my feelings are not welcome
where life and truth are replaced by having to believe

I cannot bear my loneliness there anymore
my screams are returned to me from your majestic walls
my loneliness echoes back at me—hits me again and again
until I sink to the ground

I cannot be your devoted believer anymore
trying to gain your mercy and benevolence, mother

I cannot be cast anymore into petrified expectations
of how I should be and what I should believe
or wear the gowns of virtue and hypocrisy to please you

I cannot die in lifeless cold relationships anymore
where there is no room for the truth, mother

I must leave you to come alive

6
approval addict

approval addict

approval, withheld with systematic cruelty
became—like water in the desert—all
that the child desperately longed for and sought

the more approval was not granted, the more the child craved it
the more insatiable became the child's thirst

obsessed with finding and gaining approval I formed myself
—as best as I could—so that I looked good in my parents' eyes

once my mother told me—*you have inherited*
all the good qualities of your father and me
while your sister got all the bad ones
even as a teenager I knew clearly
no one is born that way, all good or all bad
this is one of the few definite thoughts of my own I do remember

incapacitated and handicapped
I was like an empty shell, filled with the expectations of others

———————

lifeless, approval-seeking ghost
your only purpose in life was to please
to please those you were told to please
above all, those perceived as authorities—as more valuable
and more important in the hierarchy than the unimportant child

in a world where the incomprehensible reality was
contempt for children—to lecture, punish, humiliate them
to make them feel worthless and wrong
everyone's obsession was—approval

little circus horse

written in Germany, 1987

nicely—the little circus horse is running her circles
bright glistening light and admiration blind her

the daring tricks are accomplished—exit—to the stable

the circus director bows—now all the glory falls upon him
everyone looks at him
how wonderfully has he trained the little horse—what a man
—with such a talented daughter

the little horse is standing lonely in the stable

how nicely—the daughter performs her artistry at the piano
sometimes—when her accomplishment is perfect
when she has played her piece of music
        by heart—without a single mistake—perfectly
the little circus horse gets a gift—not sugar, oh no
nothing that she really desires
nothing she truly wants, oh no
she is allowed to amass a collection
of carved wooden bears her father brings home from his trips

wooden bears mean nothing to the daughter
but the attention and praise of her father
mean everything in the world to her
for a moment of admiration—for a delusion—she sells her soul
without knowing it

the little circus horse says that she loves the bears
and displays them proudly
but later—the daughter destroys them

the starving lion and the lonely snail

kept away from her parents the child starved for their attention
longed for them to notice her
without the utterance of a single word she learned
to sense her parents' expectations like a seismograph
she devoured spoken and unspoken expectations
like a hungry lion—as if meat had been thrown in front of her

often she had to fight with her brothers and sisters
trying to grab the morsels
in order to survive she had to hold onto something—anything
that would provide attention, appease her insatiable hunger
life was a hunt for expectations
to fulfill them gave her life meaning

but too many—and conflicting—expectations overwhelmed her
no way to fulfill them all—she did not know who she was anymore
—so a different force steps in to rule her
one who hates the hunt for the gold of approval
who wants to be left alone
who hates all human contact—it brings nothing but problems

this part of her withdrew from people into silence
wanted no relationships—did not wish to talk with anyone
the teenager was infamous for withdrawing into silence for days
she crawled like a snail into a protective shell—hid behind books
after her confirmation, at fourteen, she got a room of her own
to get away from her family meant freedom from expectations
meant peace and a vague, gentle contact with herself

far away from her family and country the adult woman fled
all expectations—she found places and people who allowed her
to breathe with her mind, her soul and her heart

the special child

"again and again her parents' pride, Barbara makes it possible"
written in 1969 by my father in my wedding journal

I was named after my father's mother—and my mother's mother
Irma—Barbara
my name held great significance for my parents

as a teenager I could build bridges to my parents
when I fulfilled their need for companionship
my talents and gentle nature allowed me to be special to them

my father was a gifted violinist
his musical mother had accompanied him on the piano
his father manipulated him away from music into business
yet my father still loved music and desired a musical companion
I became his accompanist
the better I played the piano
the more my father played music, and spent time, with me
sometimes we would sight-read late into the night whatever
we could find—Mozart, Schubert, Beethoven, Brahms, Kreisler

the hours I spent as a teenager making music with my father
brought happiness and pride to my childhood
gave me a sense of competence, worth, importance
of being special to him
music replaced feelings and closeness—became my life force
my strong musical bond with my father helped cover the incest
and foster a blind idealization of him

my mother's unhappiness was painful for me
I became my mother's companion during many evenings
filled with long conversations deep into the night

my mother read with dedicated interest
modern literature and liberal political magazines
my father had no interest in either

with my mother I learned to be an understanding listener
I became skilled at keeping conversations interesting and alive
as I shouldered a responsibility that was not mine
to reach my lonely mother—to alleviate her suffering
we talked about religion, history, politics and books
but not ourselves—the personal was excluded
unbeknownst to me I carried a burden
that could not be delivered but buried me deeper and deeper
in the addiction of trying to save others

I was proud to ease her loneliness and to nurture her
to provide a sense of acceptance and connection for her

those long talks made me feel important
even special and chosen—but the responsibility
to relieve my mother's misery weighed heavily
deep down I resented it strongly—and longed
for a content and self-confident mother

although I returned to visit my family for many years
I left—after I married when I was barely nineteen years old—
these conversations with my mother behind
together with all ties to organized religion

my unconscious knew about the unbridgeable abyss
between my mother and me
and guided me away from her more and more forcefully

but the young woman was unaware
she was proud to be the daughter her mother desired
it gave her life meaning and importance

competitive madness

in an atmosphere of fierce competition
we children had to work hard to be "the best"
to always attempt to be "better than the others"
like dogs fighting over a rare bone
it became a merciless struggle among us to get parental approval
to be allowed to spend a little time or to do something with them
to get them to praise us—to receive the glance of recognition

this mad fight was encouraged in cruel ways by parents
whose main concern was
what do other people think? what will the family say?
what makes a good impression? what increases our status?

parents who had gained power over dependent approval-seekers
despised and fought with contempt
their vulnerable children's desperate need for approval
although all life and all relationships
any sense of value and worth
were based upon approval

with breathtaking indifference and cruelty
one child was set up against the other

the mother fiercely favored the child who told her
what she wanted to hear—who saw the world with her eyes
who obeyed unconditionally and was loyally on her side

to move outside of these parameters meant certain exile

just the mother's words—*you are not my little darling anymore*
your sister is my favorite now
were enough to banish the left-out child into loneliness

so did the actions and attitude of a father who placed value
only on performing perfectly and winning
and who treated his sons like gods

abandoned, the girl watched powerlessly
as her mother
demonstrated triumphantly closeness with another child
        who gladly replaced the now useless child
as her father walked to the tennis court
        to show off the child he believed would help him win

her father focused on and spent time with whomever he favored
to help him gain glory in the world—above all his sons

the child stood outside—forced to watch with powerless rage
how others took what she believed to be her special place

the child—fallen out of favor and grace—was split in two

towards the outside world
the approval addict presented the desired appearance
while deep inside a giant of resentment began to grow
against this insane system of unjust, arbitrary favoritism

this furious giant could not wait to steer this life on a different path
it desired profoundly for herself—Barbara—to be recognized
for who she truly was

when this giant came out
it showed her a different perspective
of what her childhood truly had been like
of the lies she believed

then she could question with outrage and pain
the cruel games that her parents had played

haunted

around me—the unbearable noise and unrest of so many children
terror, reprimands and orders hit me like machine guns' salvos
no space, no room, no place just for me—to hide
to be alone—to escape—to find peace

persecuted by my mother's harsh and strict voice
trembling from anxiety when I hear steps approaching
tortured by punishments and beatings
I spend my days fearfully in the jail of my childhood

it is so unbearable to live there that I must cry and cry
that I must hate the people I want to love
but I may not cry—and no one cares how unbearably I suffer
and I must not hate—and how I hate that I feel hate
how I hate to be at hate's mercy

life is too hard—I am in such pain—without comfort
no room for me—my needs—my life

I hate the guards who run this prison
I hate my life in this jail—and I hate life so much
I want to run out of that house, called my home, screaming
screaming out my pain, my despair, my hatred, my misery
but—this is home—where can I go?
who would listen to or believe me—much less help me?

I cry myself to sleep and send my pain away
I put my hatred under the covers of silence

7
the eldest

harbor

the child needs a harbor to sail into, to rest, to feel at home
but mine is getting full
one—two—three—four—and five
more and more brothers and sisters fill it
my first sister arrives the day after my first birthday

pushed out—petrified
the eldest abides at the entrance
no more room for me

words—expectations
poured out over her—*'be reasonable'*—*'role model'*
'sacrifice'—*'loving kindness'*—*'share'*

they hit her like lashes of the whip
become hard, heavy rocks that block her entrance to the harbor

raging fury and jealousy
awaken hatred in the child banned from the harbor
whose loneliness—whose longing for arms to hold her
go unheard

burning pain kindles flames of despair that erupt
and bring out the wish to hurt and destroy those other ships
sink them—throw them out
so that the harbor again is mine

the good girl murders her screams with silence and by being nice
she never is angry or complains
but heeds faithfully her duties as the perfect eldest child

the fire

once at Christmas a fire broke out
in the living room—where the Christmas tree was standing
and where all the gifts had been unwrapped and were still around

my mother was the last to leave the room
she forgot to extinguish a candle
that stood behind a transparent image with a nativity scene
lit up and made visible by the light of the candle
but when the candle fell into the nativity
flames erupted—climbed up the curtain behind it
and a fire spread in the Christmas room
firemen had to come to extinguish it

I was a teenager—thirteen years old
terrified I had run up and down the stairs again and again
down—because I wanted to get out of a house on fire
but then
I ran back up again
—because the door to the room with the fire
was at the bottom of the stairs on the ground floor
I had to pass the scary door
run by the burning living room
to get to the front door through the big entrance hall
and then out of the house

I did not dare to pass that door

———————————

the family gathered at the dinner table the day after the fire
I was the only one
to be criticized by my father in front of the whole family
unforgettable—with burning shame

as if the fire continued within me
this memory—burnt into my brain—
tormented every cell of my body for years
until in therapy I felt compassion
for the teenager
afraid for her life—then—and from her earliest beginnings—
and understood her dilemma

the only one to be reprimanded was the eldest
as my father mocked my fear
how anxious and scared Barbara was
      she ran up and down the staircase
      like a frightened chicken
      how brave the younger sister
      who found the telephone number of the fire department

thus the fire was summed up by the powerful patriarch

all the blame and guilt were heaped upon the eldest
while her parents were exempted

there was no criticism for a mother
whose carelessness had started the fire
or for a father who did not bother
to help his frightened child out of a burning house

no wondering about adults
who needed a child's help to call the fire department

on the pedestal

written in Germany, fall of 2002

frightened—helpless—stretched out—flat on my tummy
I am lying high on a small plateau that barely surrounds me
and drops down steeply onto another plateau
from which again a steep escarpment is dropping
I try to get up—but when I put down my right foot
I break the ground beneath it
as if it was an artificial cardboard floor
no firm ground under my feet—no room to move
if I move—I will fall off the plateau—I do not dare to move

my dream fills me with hopeless fear
I have no clue how to get out of this predicament
I see no stairs—no rocks—no way to climb down
isolated and lonely I am stuck up there with no way out

this scary dream reveals the hopeless predicament
of the family showpiece—the eldest
positioned high above her brothers and sisters
she has to shine for her family
with her talents she has to produce great achievements
for which she then is envied and resented—even by her parents

her task is to guarantee her family's honor
to be something **special**—her parents' pride—
yet at the same time she is told over and over again
> *don't think that you are anything special*
> *who do you think you are?*
> *don't make your brothers and sisters feel bad*
> *don't be conceited—don't show off*
secretly everyone is waiting—or even wishes for her
to fall off the pedestal and crash

harbor revisited

when I am a mother myself
the old scream erupts where it should never have
with the one person I never wanted to hurt—with my own child

as I see my older child in danger of hurting the younger one
I turn into a raging monster
and find myself hitting my oldest son who is three years old

I abhorred physical violence—and still do
I was determined to be a gentle guide for my children
I wanted to treat them with kindness and respect
I longed to create love

but in that moment old denied pain took over
it assumed that my son wanted to do
what the agony of being replaced so many times
had made me desire long ago—to kill my brothers and sisters
instead of resolving the situation with love
I scream at my son—and I beat my son
by attacking him I murder my own buried scream

denial and repression stop me from being a benign role model
who gently clarifies and eases the situation
who protects the younger child
who simply points out that something dangerous might happen
who pays supportive attention to the older child
and helps him with understanding guidance to do something else

I persecute my child—to silence the dormant scream
long forgotten—I did not even recognize it as my own
when it erupted with violence

my son, never beaten before, breaks into inconsolable crying

he is so upset that he gasps for air and has trouble breathing
his face turns purple
deeply sorry, I kneel next to him
but I cannot comfort him or ease his screams for a long time

as I am confronted with my son's serious pain
the cruelty of my horrible raging act is revealed to me
deepest regret, shame and sorrow fill me
and I know—a deep trust has been broken
forever
between me and my son

———————————

years later the resurgent scream appears again
as I must face my first husband's adultery
old painful jealousy takes over
and renders me at first incapable of recognizing the truth
about myself and my marriage
for too long I cannot question or confront a husband
whom I blindly considered my harbor

as I create a harbor inside
I am able to comfort the old pain
and find the strength to leave a marriage
where the bride had a foreboding she could not decipher
—that with this man she would not find
the emotional, mental and physical closeness she longed for
and that honesty would not be welcome

it took a long time to admit to myself
that there was no room in this marriage for change and growth
that my true Self was not welcome
I learned that I could be only as close to someone
as he or she is close to him or her Self

with the old jealousy I left my first marriage behind
to set out on my own path into life

leading role

in a dream after my return from Chicago
I am the singer of Elisabeth
the leading female role in Wagner's opera *Tannhäuser*

to deliver Tannhäuser from his alleged sins
Elisabeth has to sacrifice herself and her life for him, selflessly
the opera portrays her as a noble and good human being

the pope who preaches forgiveness
does not forgive Tannhäuser his sins—joy of sensuality and sex
Tannhäuser is the bad guy—the ultimate sinner
who can never be forgiven

in the third act of the opera Elisabeth must die for his sins
and thus Tannhäuser fortunately finds salvation after all
> while I sing Elisabeth in my dream
> I decide during the second intermission
> that I do not want to continue singing this role anymore
> I don't like it
>
> I walk away from the opera
> I simply go home
> only at home do I realize—without any fear, anguish or guilt
> that the opera cannot be completed without me
> because no one is left—to die for Tannhäuser in the third act

since my return after six years in the United States
> and my initial eighteen months of therapy
I am hurt with reproachful hostility by my mother and family
they cannot understand why I do not play my old role anymore

but I have figured out that no one has to die
if I don't sing and act anymore as everyone expects me to

why did Wagner believe—what a destructive and horrible belief—
that salvation can be gained only
through giving up on your Self and your life?

_____

why do Christians believe that salvation can only be achieved
through the death of another human being—God's own son?

wouldn't God have other means—and more power and wisdom
to forgive humanity's sins than to bring salvation to mankind
through his own son's death?

do we idealize the sacrifice of a child
—brought about through the wish or actions of its parents—
as a symbol for the pain, the martyrdom and self-sacrifice
that too many children must suffer?

what would happen if we treated each child as a child of God
as Jesus' parents did
with true respect, supportive reverence and sincere devotion?
without physical, emotional or mental violence?

children who grow up in the spirit of understanding and love
for themselves and for others
will live and spread it

they will appreciate their lives and those of others

children who grow up without violence and cruelty
without uselessly inflicted pain
will not have the need to hurt others
        to find salvation through self-sacrifice
                or to resolve conflicts through violence

8
tyrant fear

Nikolaus

December 6, Nikolaus day—a nightmare of sheer terror
outside it is dark
the children are gathered in the living room, waiting fearfully
finally the doorbell rings—it rings forever—long and longer
heavy, forceful, violent, loud, threatening boot-steps
stomp into the house
the children anticipate with increasing horror

a terrifying man called Nikolaus enters the living room
a bearded man with a heavy coat and a sack on his back
a rod in his hand—terror petrifies the children—they hide
under their father's desk—while grownups smile all-knowingly

Nikolaus also brings along two books, one golden, the other black
aloud and forcefully—in a strict tone of voice
he reads from them about each individual child

if you are written up in the black book—you are a bad child
you are scolded and criticized in front of everyone
maybe even judged as so evil
that Nikolaus may have to take you away
seven years old, I appear in the black book—reprimanded
for skipping—merrily down the street

written up in the golden book—you are a good child
you feel special, like a role model—your parents are proud of you
but you are envied and resented by your brothers and sisters
so you feel saved—but isolated, lonely and sad

the terror eases when the sack is emptied
nuts and fruits, some sweets, spill out on the ground
we may pick them up
Nikolaus and the heavy loud steps leave

chaos

chaos ruled a childhood marked by unpredictability and hatred
the chaos around her created chaos inside her

mercilessness and coldness
arbitrary persecution
neglect and abandonment

struggling against the crazy and horrifying chaos around her
the powerless child fought for her survival

her inner chaos of fear reflected the chaos of her outer reality

the horrifying outer chaos
—disguised as and even called love—
formed her inner world
filled it with confusion, guilt and anxiety
inescapable loneliness
turned it into a chaos of wounds and screams

the chaos inside and out
      only told her of her failure
            convinced her of her inborn guilt
                  declared her utter evilness
                        confirmed her lack of worth

and she believed it all

tin soldier

stiff—petrified—I follow the rules

kept in line and oppressed by guilt
with a broken backbone—replaced by wires of obedience
I emerge—a perfectly functioning robot—a shining tin soldier
everything of my own—any self-expression
forbidden—judged as wrong
my truth—condemned and persecuted like a crime

constant judgments of my guilt and evilness strike me with terror
burn into every cell the inescapable feeling of—*I am wrong*

fear and guilt are the mad allies
that produce a dangerously loyal vassal
and turn me into a rigid Prussian tin soldier
obedient, submissive, mouth-less, voice-less, spine-less
inflexible, "upright," very functional—without making problems

my humanity crippled—only my deepest fear and obsession
I am wrong and I do everything wrong
burns and scorches inside

I can ease this inner hell only if I function perfectly
according to the authorities in my life—parents, family, god
teachers, husband, employers, governments, states

what has become of me? who am I?

a slave in bondage—a timid serf—submissive and servile
frozen Into a non-being without integrity, conscience, a center
who despises herself over and over again for her cowardice

77

I won't let go

we are out sailing—but the joyful trip
has become a frightening struggle to survive
the sailboat has turned over in a storm
filled with water it is lying on its side—drifting in a stirred-up sea
we cannot bring it back up

my father and sister are sitting on the exposed side of the boat
my brother and his friend stand on the mast floating on the water
I am in the water holding onto the rudder
I am supposed to turn the boat into the wind should it come up

I am in the water for an endless time
wave after wave rolls over me—my will to live disappears
I feel the desire to let go of the boat
to just drift away with the waves
my strength to withstand them is vanishing
I want to die

but I have two young children
I think of them—how can I let go
I cannot abandon them—I must live
my children need me—so I dare to speak up
I tell my brother that I need to sit on the boat too
        I cannot drift in the stormy sea anymore
and—I may sit on the boat

_____

the teenager once broke down laughing uncontrollably
when she heard the joke of a mother
who does not want her unborn child to live
so she follows her doctor's advice
and eats ice, lots of it, constantly—upon the next visit

the doctor is surprised to find the child still alive
as he observes mother and child through an x-ray machine
the child in the womb clasps her arms around herself
over and over again—and with every move she says
hang in there—hang in there—persevere

––––––––––––––

how did the child, without letting go, survive wave after wave
of physical violence, accusations, condemnations
of hostile threats and deadly fear, torture and persecution?

how did the child, without giving up, survive
storm after storm of being blamed and judged
humiliated and punished
being put down and mocked with derision?

she drifted back and forth between hope and despair
they became the emotional poles of her life

when she gained what she considered love
she would get her head above water again
and ride back on the wave of hope into life

when worthlessness overwhelmed her
she submerged in that devastating darkness
where her wish to live vanished and all she could think was
I cannot live like that anymore
I want to be dead
please, let me die—this life is too hard
I want to let go

––––––––––––––

many times the child's ordeal haunted the grownup woman
made her wish to leave this life behind

my love of life and of my children—and my friendships
gave me the strength to hold on
provided my determination—I won't let go

confirmation

religion was of the greatest importance to my mother
as a small child I was indoctrinated with religious horrors
which claimed that God saw everything
children's books with pictures of the devil were read to me
they made me believe that hell existed
and filled me with terror I would end up there if I made a mistake

at my confirmation at fourteen
I was told that I now was an adult member of the church
I regarded this as a new expectation and duty I had to fulfill
and took it seriously to please my mother

on the day of my confirmation
the girls wore black dresses and the boys black suits
we looked terribly serious, as if we were attending a funeral

in the afternoon, surrounded by family, festivities, precious gifts
I cried—no one knew what was wrong with me
neither did I

in therapy my confirmation came up as a painful memory
that revealed that I had to sacrifice my Self
to have a relationship with my mother

my mother was so deeply different from me
an unbridgeable abyss divided us
but I wanted to reach her—I longed to build bridges to her
so I felt obligated to enter her world—religion

to make her proud of me I identified with her religion

following my confirmation
I taught children in two different Sunday schools

and often attended the service for adults too

my soul cried that day—without my conscious awareness—
because my mother's religion and her way of life
were not my home

her dark world where terror and fear reigned
meant death for the alive child within me
for my true Self

my father—his presence—his world—meant life to the child

I cried because I had to give up who I truly was
and what I really cared about
so that I could build a bridge to my mother

as the family showpiece
I became her very special, irreplaceable daughter
the chosen child

when this child began to recognize and speak her truth
the bridge of fear
the bridge that I had built through self-denial
collapsed
the abyss between us became visible
and could never be bridged again

life and death

Germany, 1985

when I return to Germany after six years abroad
I must live close to my parents again
the first year has passed—I am thirty-five years old

before a summer trip my parents come to visit
my mother catches me alone in the kitchen—with her bitter voice
she reproachfully pours her poison of guilt over me
now that you don't take care of me anymore
I at least had expected you to take care of your sick, old father

stunningly to both of us
my reaction is not fear or obedient submission anymore
but anger, which lets me say quietly but firmly
my relationship with my father is my own business
and I cannot have any more personal conversations with you

my husband wonders why my mother has left crying
and why he can see hatred in my eyes

but then the terror of the child returns—I dared to contradict
I tremble from severe anxiety all night—I cannot sleep
no tranquilizer can calm the terror upsetting every cell of my body
and I remember expressing early in therapy
that there is a fight for life and death between my mother and me

in the morning, after a sleepless night, my father calls
Ritzka, how are you—is all he says

upon hearing his voice and these words
my trembling, terrorized cells calm down
all my fear disappears instantly as I am filled with the security
that I can disagree with my mother—and am safe

the Jew in the family

at the beginning of my therapy
I talked often about the Jews and the Nazis
until my therapist suggested—*you felt like a Jew in your family*
from then on I began to talk about myself

I felt understood because so often a feeling overwhelmed me
I am the cause for all the problems in the world

only children were blamed and punished
only they seemed to make mistakes
only children had to constantly say—*I am sorry*
and ask for forgiveness
only children were made feel guilty and responsible
for the problems in their lives—and even for those
that occurred around them

as a child—and after the incest—and after the car accident
I had as the scapegoat, as the person to blame
for the horrible things that happened to me
only myself

I was trained to believe that parents were always right—infallible
like gods—who could do no wrong
a child was nothing but a dumping ground for guilt and blame

I am the cause for all the problems in the world
I believed and felt like that for most of my life
because the child was treated as the cause for every problem
blamed and pronounced guilty day in and day out
preached to zealously, condemned and accused relentlessly

any problem that occurred in my life or around me
used to terrify me and send me to a state of such petrified fear

that it made me incapable of thinking about solutions
my brain collapsed as if short-circuited
my mind circled hopelessly—like a broken record—
between the problem and my guilt that had brought it on

I felt like a desperate insane person rocking in mental anguish

endlessly I tried to find a way out—which I never did
no one helped me find it
problems or conflict were nothing but opportunities
to blame and to punish
to make a show of parental power and might

they never were chances to help and support a child
to teach her how to approach and resolve a problem
to strengthen her confidence and skills

as body and brain trembled with chaotic terror
the child's system broke down
mired in fear and hopelessness

to be the cause for all the problems in the world
is that what being a Jew
in the hell of anti-semitism
feels like?

9
in between

at the dinner table

at one end of the table my father—at the other my mother
in between three children—sitting on each side of the table
my place was at my father's side

I watch my father
he shovels his own, special food into his mouth
rarely looks up—rarely says a word
and regularly dribbles his food down his front

I observe my mother at the other end
she constantly criticizes her children and demands
   sit straight—hands on the table
   don't talk with a full mouth! behave yourselves better!
   don't spill! don't dribble! don't wiggle your chairs!
   don't, don't, don't
her constant criticism often grows into yelling
until she leaves the table furiously
the meal and the joy of sharing food—ruined

how confusing and painful it was to sit in between them
to look back and forth
I looked to the right—I looked to the left—is life about
how my father lives—or how my mother tells us to be?

I watched my parents just as helplessly
as my mother saved every penny
   bought the cheapest, most unappealing food
   only basic necessities—with the reasoning
   that one has to be prepared for wars
     when one might lose everything
   often there was barely enough food for all the children
   then we fought over it

I saw how my father spent money lavishly
  he did not seem to have any limits
  came home with trays of fruits and cake
  he brought home delicious things
  there was enough good food for all of us
  he took us out for wonderful meals
  then we had fun times together

one parent was a religious fanatic
the other avoided church and prayed in nature
one was afraid and hated to travel
the other traveled all the time and loved the world
one despised
good food, nice clothes, going out
while the other enjoyed
dressing well, smelling good and eating well

my heart sank—my soul filled with sadness
as I looked powerlessly back and forth between my parents
with my head spinning
wondering
how shall I live—what is the right way?

the photo

my mother came from a blue-blooded, noble family
and an extremely rich background—but was trained to be modest
unassuming—and to never show wealth
my father came from a bourgeois family of tradespeople
who lived voluptuously, joyfully, loudly and enjoyed their wealth

on a photo my father must have made one New Year's Eve
we children, our mother and my father's mother
are arranged behind a big table decorated with festive splendor
big bottles of champagne—big plates filled with fruits and cookies
colorful crackers—my father loved to create this table
he spent most of the day building it for the evening
when relatives, a musical family, would come to visit

we spent the last evening of the year making music
everybody who played an instrument performed something
I have fond memories of my joy and excitement
when chamber music was played later in the evening

my father took this photo before the guests arrived
my mother looks aside furiously and with contempt
all the children have frozen, terrified expressions in their faces
except for me—I am the only one smiling

our eyes are filled with visible fear
my grandmother's eyes are turned upward—askew with horror
as if trying to leave this horrible scene
her face looks sad and frightened

no one looks at my father except his oldest son

what do these horrified expressions mean?
clearly a bad fight preceded this photo

my mother did not like this table—she battled anything
that she considered luxurious or unnecessary

when we were little children she battled my father
for taking us out for tea and cake on Sundays
my mother was so furious about it that she did not come along
but stayed behind, alone at home
she believed he spoiled her children

my mother had violent outbreaks of rage and anger
towards all of us
here she must have accused and yelled at my father
for creating this festive table—for "showing off"

it is heartbreaking to see these terrified eyes
to discover the horror in the children's faces

I remember what it felt like to be with this angry woman
whose bitter, accusatory, judgmental attitude and tone
was our daily bread
it ruined all joy of life

it felt as if life and happiness were systematically eradicated
with a fire extinguisher of verbal and physical attacks

my father did not protect us from her aggressiveness
and once, in my thirties, I asked him why
he said that he did not know about it—this from a man
who said that the Germans knew what happened to the Jews

why am I smiling in this photo?
early in therapy I once said
if the world went down—I would still smile at my father

broken heart—twisted heart

my father is a man my mother does not want me to love
in my presence she puts him down, talks badly about him
and I feel it is a crime to love my father—to be close to him
with every scathing remark about him
I feel as if warmth and love in my heart disappear
while my longing for a loving connection grows
and searches desperately for someone to love and who loves me

what have you done to my heart, mother?
what business do you have talking about my father in a way
that makes me feel I should despise, even hate him?

why do you make me feel it is a crime to love him?
why do you portray him as a worthless failure I should spurn?
why do you want to hurt my relationship with him?
are you jealous of any closeness around you?
can you not bear to witness love around you
just as you cannot tolerate any sign of life and truth around you?

you demand my attention exclusively for yourself

with the poison of anger, bitterness, contemptuous accusations
your guilt-inducing tactics extinguish life and love around you

why do your words have such power over me
that I cannot follow my heart but have to crawl in your footsteps
into your maze of hatred—into your spider net of guilt?
you have turned love into a curse—you have broken my heart
I cannot love freely and with joy because my heart
has been programmed not to love when I feel love

bound by chains of pity, duty, loyalty, sacrifice and false gratitude
I was tied to you by obligational dependency—but not by love

in between

my father despises with ridicule or outright contempt
my mother's family's more humble and simple way of life
they are more idealistic and intellectual
more religious and quiet
my mother hates with furious passion
the way my father and his family live
they are emotional—what a horrible thing
live visibly wealthy lives
and—what hypochondriac weaklings they are—
they make such a fuss about nothing—they even get sick

———————————

I see the child in between these two extreme poles
lost between polarized worlds
I see her standing there—watching a mad game of mind-tennis
in which poisonous balls—*my way of life is better than yours*
are volleyed back and forth

the child's head swivels back and forth
her soul is torn apart while she wonders
whom shall I follow? why do they hate each other so?
filled with desperate confusion, flooded with anxiety
she feels dizzy, completely lost, abandoned and lonely

during certain times of her life this child follows her mother
and turns into a very religious teenager
but religion does not ease her anxieties and pain
on the contrary—religion makes her feel false and hypocritical
so later she avoids churches
drifts into a superficial enjoyment of luxuries
which leaves her empty and unfulfilled

as the good wife who is now her husband's showpiece
shopping becomes her distraction from her inner emptiness

the child's mind, split into either/or
continues the combat she was exposed to as a child
long into adulthood

the child cannot find a resolution
helpless to reconcile her polarized life experiences
she cannot create peace and harmony within herself
she cannot figure out how to live

as she tries to discover what makes a good person
she looks back and forth
—at her mother
—at her father
but there is no answer

life is to her
nothing
but the agony
of being torn apart

how can I love?

how can I love a mother who demands to own me?
who regards my unconditional loyalty as her birthright?
who considers any thought deviant from her ideology
as blasphemy?
how can I love a mother who is capable
of intentionally destroying
the truth, love and relationships?

how can I love my father if he does not protect me?
if it is a crime to have a connection with him?
if he worships his sons?
if he sarcastically mocks the child
brutally puts down the teenager—and sexually abuses her?

I bleed where love was meant to be in my heart
while a devouring longing for a loving connection
burns painfully in my body

love meant degrading, hopeless dependency and pain
love was a nightmare
I had no experiences with love
I had no clue what love was all about

I followed blindly destructive patterns
—imprinted early in my life—
about love
          as blind pity and unconditional loyalty
          as devoted dependence and obedient adoration
          as submissive servitude

patterns that I paid for through self-denial

10
battlefield child

battlefield child

old wars are continued and fought
on the battlefield child
I am the battlefield of such old fights

I symbolize a powerful god
whose unconditional approval is sought yearningly
as my parents' eyes search my eyes
with the desperate longing of two children who did not know love
and—long—to get it from me

I symbolize the old enemy
who evokes memories of my parents' pasts
all sorts of feelings that could not live with their own parents
can come alive with me—buried feelings of longing and despair
of hatred and revenge—of retaliation and boundless rage
can at long last surface and be released
without fear and with a clear conscience

the powerlessness of childhood
transformed to boundless power through parenthood

I symbolize a dangerous opponent
whose otherness cannot be tolerated
punitive actions—furious looks—judgmental blaming
invade and occupy the mind and soul of the child
every reproachful look damns me, even years later as an adult
back into the old submission

I represent a mirror, too
where my parents need to see beautiful reflections of themselves
to give them the experience of pride and glory

I am the redeemer who has to satisfy their longing for recognition

as my parents internal view goes back in time with despair
am I the most beautiful in your eyes, mother, father?

on the battlefield of old fights
I become a powerless puppet between my parents
in my mother's mind I am her possession as well as her rival
with disparaging remarks she drives wedges into relationships
sends the message—*you may not love others
it is wrong to love others—you must love only me*
the child learns to hide feelings of love even from herself

the final battle
the devastating blow on the battlefield child
her beloved father seduces the teenage child to be his lover
makes her the intruder into her parents' marriage

the battlefield child is crushed—nothing left of her
except the conviction that she is a worthless whore
a sinful monster who brought this disaster upon herself

filled with unbearable guilt and burning shame
the girl vanishes on the battlefield

only parts of her are left, scattered and broken

these different identities try to run her life as best as they can
the battle has entered the girl
all that the struggling states of her mind can do is
fight over the best survival strategies
she cannot organize the chaos inside
with its firm hold on her and its control over her life

her true Self cannot help her
it was the battlefield's victim

no one there to help her reclaim it

the army of the believers

you, my parents, are soldiers in the army of fanatics
who want to exorcise the devil of contradiction out of the child
who want to beat down and silence
the enemy—different thinking and the truth

I cannot speak my truth
if I am sad, I hear—*pull yourself together*
when I express my love—*stop that monkey love*
I do well in school and I am proud—*don't be so full of yourself*
I have an opinion—*who do you think you are*

"conform" is the command
at first my mother leads this fight
in my teenage years my father takes over the army command
and enforces his ideology

the victim who blocks the army's path with truth
is attacked with blame—battled with fanatic cruelty
tortured with guilt and isolation

this army marches solidly behind their leader's belief
only one true belief may exist for this army—that of parents
this belief unites the army

I see this army marching towards me, ready to attack
I step aside—I avoid them

fanatically these soldiers march on—straight ahead
following their belief
they are so busy believing that they don't see me
they won't miss me in their army—they don't like non-believers

I wait until they have passed by—and behind them I discover life

brainwashed

you invade my mind with a vengeance
as if it was yours—your exclusive and sole possession

your beliefs take over the child's dependent, powerless brain
as if it was your unquestionable right to live there
you believe I should see the world with your eyes
you believe I should agree with you

my brain—malleable receiver of your commands and beliefs

you don't want to know what lives in my mind
you want me to be a devoted believer of your every word
deeply have you ingrained into me
that your enemies have to be mine
that I must hate whom you hate—that I must look arrogantly
down upon those who don't have "the right belief"

you are not teaching me to see or to think for myself
you are forcing me to believe
you are not teaching me to love but to judge and condemn

why do you want lies to occupy my brain and confuse my mind?
how can I distinguish between reality and lies
when to you it is a sin to expose lies and to live in truth?

you are my parents
my love for you is the unconditional
all-forgiving, all-understanding love of a child

what unimaginable power you have over my mind

trapped

to experience love for a lover made me feel trapped
as if I had no way out, as if stuck in a place with no room for me
where I was not welcome—yet not allowed to leave
when I used to experience love
I felt I was suffocating, as if I could not breathe
as if someone else took up all the air—none left for me

shoved off to different nurses—three in the first year of my life—
my experiences with my parents had been a trap
a devastating mixture of feeling unimportant and worthless
of being treated without respect
the child depended for her survival on two unpredictable enemies
who called cruelty and derision—"for your own good"

to "love" had meant
to be in danger, to suffer without dignity and rights
to always be on high alert—on guard for the next catastrophe
the child had learned to fear love
as a treacherous, deceitful game that she would never trust

obedience, fear and submission meant love to the child
feeling trapped and longing for freedom were tied to love
how I longed to get out of that house—that kind of "love"
that impenetrable, unalterable darkness
how I yearned to be free
what I believed to be love kept me chained to parents
who had turned my introduction to love into a nightmare from hell

when the adult woman realized her fate
she left it all behind and found relationships
where truth and caring mattered
kindness, openness and honesty were appreciated
and where closeness, truth and vitality were welcome

no place for me

in a wild, roaring ocean of fear—stirred up restlessly
I am looking for an island of love

in my desperate fight for survival I look for a lap
where protection, warmth, tranquility and kindness will hold me
where I can feel at home—experience understanding and peace
a place just for me—my place
but around me is chaos—hordes of others
more and more brothers and sisters are chasing—replacing me

the hunter is blowing his cruel horn for the battle
to win the currency of love
the greatest self-denial wins the biggest smile
this highest price is paid without hesitation
just to be able to somehow reach the godlike parents

I try my best
I fight hard to survive this merciless, humiliating hunt
but the hordes of brothers and sisters are always
hard on my heels
they try to survive the deadly game too—they push me aside

I fight bitterly, with meanness, to find a place for me
using any miserable weapon, any trick I can think of
obliterating my honesty, my integrity, my truth

yet somehow I am aware of what I am doing
I despise what I am turning into
I hate myself for what I am capable of doing
in order to find
what I was not granted—what I could not find:
my place

11
extinguishing a woman

"Yet pre-feminism, a Freudian bias eroticized incest as a fantasy of the victim, while class bias depicted it as an immorality of the poor. In fact, part of Freud's reason for abandoning his interest in the sexual abuse of children was society's hostility to the idea that many abusers were solid patriarchs of the middle and upper classes, not to mention the possibility of Freud's reluctance to believe it of his own childhood.

"We also know that the greater the imbalance of power—between the genders as elsewhere—the greater the abuse. In families where men are captains of industry and finance in the outside world, the internal power differences between men and women are extreme, and men's sense of being able to do no wrong is often greater than elsewhere. So is the reluctance of authorities to intervene. Furthermore, children are more likely to be isolated, cared for by servants who may be passing on their own abuse or acting out a resentment of wealth itself. Many observers believe that sexual abuse is MORE prevalent among families of inherited wealth and power than in the population at large—and I agree."

Gloria Steinem, "The Masculinization of Wealth," *Moving Beyond Words:*
Age, Rage, Sex, Power, Money, Muscles: Breaking the Boundaries of Gender

"What Steinem had come to realize. . . was how intensely many rich women have internalized their assigned role in paternalistic, patriarchal families, how deeply incapable they are, by and large, of questioning, let alone changing, their subordinate roles, how little money, apart from credit cards, they actually have in their own power to spend, and, above all, how likely they are to have been abused and sexually assaulted in childhood in their families, in which the difference between women and men was often greater than in poor or middle class families."

Carolyn G. Heilbrun, *The Education of a Woman: The Life of Gloria Steinem*

revisiting the Queen Mary—at the scene of the crime

Los Angeles, April 2001

for Earl

I have returned to the room where my father
manipulated my love for him, exploited my obedience
and raped me

my mind kept the memory of this crime from me
for thirty-three years—to save my sanity

taken on an exciting dream journey by her father
the sixteen-year-old teenager—proud and exuberant
thought it a miracle to have her father to herself
they traveled from Europe to the United States
on a great ship called the Queen Mary
where they shared a cabin—in this cabin I have lit a candle

I have returned to the scene of the crime thirty-five years later
with four letters I have written to face this scary place
with a sculptured bird from my therapist's office
with Kleenex, a candle, paper, a pen, and an empty box
and with a man at my side who loves me

the bird is my symbol for my spirit
it was imprisoned in this cabin for all those years
I had to leave it behind on this ship
because my father took it away from me here in this room

the journey to reclaim my spirit has been long and difficult
like an explorer who travels into an impenetrable, scary jungle
and encounters terrifying adventures and dangerous obstacles
I have traveled into my mind, soul and body to arrive at the truth
to find my history and the causes for my suffering

yesterday I read in tears four letters in this room
one to my mother—one to my father
one to the sixteen-year-old Barbara who trusted her father
one to the man at my side who welcomes my search for the truth

today I put these letters into the empty box to take them home
they are the utterances of my silenced voice, of my lost spirit
with whom I am reunited in this room

the scene of the crime is now an empty room
the candle shining on the table
I am sitting on the bed
where my life and my mind lost their direction and power
where my own father took away from me
what his presence in my life had preserved for so long
my connectedness with life
I shed tears for a life that could not be fulfilled
I thank those who helped me face and bear the truth

the poisonous magic of a monstrous promise
—kept faithfully for all those years by a most loyal child—
and the curse of an evil crime with devastating consequences
have been broken
the power of a demonic spell, which darkened my soul and mind
has been defused

life is mine now—to live

I greet and welcome my passionate, inquisitive, thoughtful
brave and adventuresome spirit
I look forward to the journey we now can make together

united we can hear my life's calling
leave the demon and the darkness behind
and follow and fulfill my destiny

three kinds of women

how I longed to leave your dishonest, cowardly world behind
and the limited, arrogant frame of mind of your class

your male arrogance held an incomprehensible view of women
whom you divided into three categories: those you don't touch
those you have sex with—and those whom you marry

full of yourself and your insane ideology
you warned me of these "three kinds of women"
in a sinister voice, over and over again
fanatically determined to make sure
that I stayed on the "right course" that would lead into marriage

you classified women by what kind of sex they offered
paid sex—or unpaid sex—or married sex
it determined in your mind a woman's destiny and worth
how dare you find only three purposes for a woman's life

in my forties and divorced
I showed a series of self-portraits to a photo class I attended
under one photo I had written your curse—I wanted to exorcise it
questions from the class—*which kind of woman did you become?*

as a teenager I had to listen to your sermon several times a year
it rolled over me with regular ferocity like a flood, year after year

you put your finger at your temple when I tried to talk to you
yet I had to listen politely to your narrow-minded bullshit
which you preached like a pope as eternal dogma

how I hated it—how I despised you
I gave up communicating with you—a man who ignored my life
to such a degree that he did not even bother to attend

my graduation, where I was a shining performer on the piano

why was it so important to you to program this curse into me?
I was taught to love and trust you
so your curse invaded me, despite my resentment
seized my brain and controlled me
          especially after you fucked me—and I had to doubt
          what kind of woman I had become
it made me your captive—it executed its destructive power
like a secret seed planted inside me that grew into an inner tyrant
who ruled my self-perception and my life
according to your plans—without my awareness

how many years was I powerless against your curse
how long did I remain at the mercy of your lies

but in my forties I furiously left behind the good daughter
like a snake abandons an old and useless skin
how shocked was I to realize that I had tried so long and hard
to fit into a skin that you designed and made me wear
it never was mine

tied no longer to the coercion
of worshiping the illusion of a benevolent father
I have freed myself from the tyranny of your curse

I have found another kind of woman—the liberated woman
her life can be anything she wants it to be
devoted to any profession
to anything and anyone she wants to devote it to
including herself

as I claim my power
I dedicate my life to nurture my true Self
and the true Selves of those I love and those I meet
and I devote my life to overcoming silences
within and around me

blindness and manipulation

"*crippled but free*
I was blind all the time I was learning to see"
the Grateful Dead

when she was sixteen a young man entered the teenager's life
quietly and gently, but also with determination
he wanted to build a real relationship with her

although he lived far away
he came almost every weekend on his bicycle to see her
they walked through forests endlessly
talking—holding and feeling each other
they found places and time to share their awakening love

her father never greeted him—her father ignored him
he never invited him into our living room
he called his daughter's boyfriend—her "kitchen-friend"

after two happy years in which a loving relationship had grown
another man came who wanted to go out with her
when he came for the first date—he entered the living room
where he sat and talked with her father
who received him like a prince already during this first visit

she was so blind that she did not see or grasp anything
she felt flattered—and wanted to get out of that dark house
away from tyrants where she felt not at home

the daughter could not consciously realize
that her father preferred the older and wealthier man
she could not see her father as a selfish liar

unaware of the sick manipulation she was falling victim to
she could not imagine that her father was only interested

in money and reputation—she could not admit
that she was just one of the "daughter cows"
to be exploited by being married off to the most promising bidder

it was unimaginable for this daughter to recognize
that she was nothing but a means to an end
that her father used her to decorate himself and his family
with the important name of this man—and his wealth

the incest memory—and all the old inner turmoil and despair
were repressed from her consciousness
she did not know how she longed to escape
and leave her misery behind—to this hidden drama
marriage seemed a way out, a chance for salvation
a promise to free her from the curse of worthlessness

to leave and live on her own was not an option
her inner chaos dreaded separations

her father ignored the man who recognized and loved her
and a relationship where love had blossomed
instead—"the right one"
      who conformed to her father's values
      who gave her father what he was after
      who guaranteed the permission to be married
entered the living room where true love was not welcome

----

forty-five years old she met a man who took joy in her
who wanted to build a loving relationship with her
he came from the "wrong" background, too
he also would not have been welcome in that living room

and it was only then that she recognized
how she had fallen victim to her father's manipulations

determined to claim life and love
she invited him into **her** living room—and into **her** life

father, unscrupulous

father—unscrupulous, cruel father
you pushed your own child into a whirl of anxiety and guilt
in which the teenager drowned and perished—unable to surface

father—without conscience
you used your child as a lover—as an unpaid whore
your crime gave my self-confidence the final blow

father—how I adored you
how unconditionally and completely I trusted you
while you split my mind into confusion and self-hatred
I could not hate you for what you did to me

father—irresponsible, brutal father
you deceived and betrayed your child unimaginably
but condemned your loyal child to silence
while you continued a monstrous life of lies and mendacity

father—hypocritical father—I cannot live a lie like you did
I am incapable of such a deceitful way of life
forgetting saved me from going crazy

father—unscrupulous father
I say goodbye to you—and to my illusions
that enabled me to believe in a loving, protecting father

father—without conscience—brutal father
this is my farewell
your betrayal of me is a crime for which you never atoned
—but it has become the source of my rebellion
the foundation for my liberation and spirited journey

father—deceitful liar—I am walking a different path

my rebellion honors the truth and serves life

I leave behind a different legacy:
this book
and a life of protest and dignity
that has overcome your crime

12
never on my side

the emperor

written in Germany, 1985

the emperor has ascended the throne one more time
she announces to the subject
>*as you don't take care of me anymore*
>*I had at least expected you*
>*to take care of my weak, old spouse*
>*your father*

hidden behind those visible words is the message
>*you don't do enough for me*
>*you are a bad subject*
>*I don't take pleasure in you anymore*
>*I condemn you—you don't live up to my expectations*

the subject is stunned
in the emperor's Reich the subject does not exist
as a human being—with the right to be herself
in this kingdom
a subject is nothing but a non-person
expected to serve and fulfill the emperor's demands

this non-person struggled to survive a most painful year
tried to find a life in the old world
and explored the possibility of somehow living
in her mother's kingdom

the subject vows to leave the kingdom
there are places in the world
where one does not have to live as subject and emperor

this is where I want to live

against me

it is the day of my fortieth birthday—I have left my marriage
I travel by myself today from Florida to Chicago
but there is a snowstorm—the plane is diverted to Milwaukee
as we come to a stop I see from my window airplanes lined up
but no terminal in sight—we are stranded out in nowhere

my eyes stare at the door of the plane which does not open
I have never experienced claustrophobia—but in this moment
it seizes me with vehemence and a vengeance
I am overwhelmed by the anguish of—*I want out*
I must get out of here—a tremendous headache hits me
and I feel a horrible pressure torturing my neck

I get my pen and notebook and write
my overwhelming feelings unfold on the paper before me
and there is only one event in my life I can tie them to—
my own birth—I was the first child—my birth took very long
anesthetized
my mother could not help me get out
I realize what it felt like to be stuck in the birth channel for hours
as endless contractions press me painfully against her

my home for nine months has become a vise

when I clearly understand what the child suffered
my protest arises—against the inhumanity of being born
without my mother's help—against doctors who abandon me
by rendering her incapable of pushing me out
against parents who let that happen
the baby is abandoned by a cold and cruel medical system
her mother's body has become her enemy

the baby's screams emerge—*I must get out of here*—*get me out*

I cannot bear being stuck in here with such unbearable pain
terrified, closed in, trapped

I write for two hours until the claustrophobia disappears
fear only returns when the pilot does not tell the truth
he announces that we will be at the gate in half an hour
but an hour later we are still out there, waiting
we are stuck for five hours in the plane, out in nowhere
I cannot even make a call to cancel my own birthday party

panicked the baby struggled to get out and survive
while her mother's body and the medical system
fought
against her
from this stressful life beginning stemmed
—imprinted deeply into her every cell—
the most difficult and terrifying feeling
you are against me—life is against me

what started out as a purely physical impression
as the body's shocking first experience when I entered this world
was reinforced deeper and stronger
with every reprimand, every attack and every beating

this fear moved from the purely physical level
through physical, verbal, emotional and mental abuse
to an overpowering wall—*my mother's body—my mother's being*
they act in hostile, dangerous and cruel ways
against my body and life—against me

as my mind became clear and my eyes opened
my mind had to accept
what my body and emotions had known all along

my mother is against me
that was the inescapable reality and truth
of my relationship with my mother

thicket in the dark forest

long ago—I just had started therapy—
I wrote a letter to my mother to explain that I had entered therapy

it was scary to tell her that something was "wrong" with me
afraid to hurt her I made this information short
and embedded it in lots of good things about me and my life
that would please her
her answer made clear that I would have to walk this path alone

I dared to respond by expressing how I felt
that there was an abyss between us
and then I wrote again lots of good things about me and my life

the abyss was always there—deathly afraid of my mother
I watched her as a child and I knew—*I never will be like you*
and yet—you were my mother—your mind was my universe
your beliefs became my religion as I was fundamentally trained
and programmed to believe and to follow you

my father focused his attention on his sons, Hotto disappeared
so you were the only one left to whom I seemed to matter

why was I so afraid to hurt you?
why did I always protect you?
why was I always concerned about you—but not myself?
why did it never bother you when you caused me pain?

I was trapped under a thicket of branches and trees
which had fallen upon me and entangled me
in a nightmarish thunderstorm of relentless persecution

I was lost in the middle of a forest where it was eternally dark
where there seemed no way out

the ticket was woven of guilt, blame, hostility and hatred
and the light of love could not enter the forest of your dark world
or penetrate the thicket of your destructive beliefs
that held me entangled for so long

one day a friend asked me—*why do you suffer?*
in an instant I knew the answer clearly
and just speaking out loud
what until then I had not even dared to think
changed my life profoundly—*I suffer because of my mother*
I suffer because my mother causes me pain
she tries to silence and extinguish me with guilt
every time I see her
that day I decided to leave the thicket and the forest

suddenly I could see that it was my mother's thicket—not mine
and all I had to do was—to crawl away from it
get out from under it, escape it
get up and leave the forest
and I did

as I got away further and further
my eyes began to see
my soul began to sing
my heart began to open
my mind began to recognize the truth—and expanded
to see reality clearly

and suddenly I was free to walk towards the light
free to live

telling the truth heals

written in 2002

I was five months eighteen
when I told my mother that I got engaged
as we walked to the favorite family restaurant by the sea
she responded—*when you speak with your father*
don't say I am engaged
you have to ask—may I please become engaged

I still see myself walking along the harbor with my father
—how I loved the harbor—the ships—the sea—
when I told him I was engaged his answer was
you have kissed someone before
you know what the great love of your life is

the following weekend my fiancé came to the island
to ask formally for my hand—as my parents had demanded

my parents asked to sleep on it
the next day they said—*you are too young, but we approve*
you can marry him—just wait a few months until the wedding

those seven months became difficult and painful
they were filled with anxiety, sleeplessness, drugs—the accident
shortly before the wedding my mother asked me one day
are you not doing well because you don't want to marry this man?

you just made sure you said something, mother
so that you would carry no responsibility for this marriage
which was so obviously a problem from the start
your question was too little—too late
you covered your traces, created an alibi
so that in the end you were without blame
because you had said something—at least once

but your question did not even scratch
the surface of the iceberg of despair built up inside of me

your question did not want an answer
it was meant to cover your traces
the truth was not your priority

years later—I was almost fifty—
the scar of my hysterectomy remained for years
a scabby crust—dark brown and ugly
called "the angry scar" by my acupuncturist

until I sent my letter to you and told you, my mother, the truth

after that the scar healed dramatically
every month more of its dark crust disappeared

you claim that I tell a lie about my father
and lecture me that speaking up is silver but silence is gold
but that is not true—to speak up brings gold
—the gold of health and sanity—
because my body healed after I told you, my own mother
the truth

it was the scariest thing I ever did
I was so used to mothering you—while taught to ignore
my need to have my mother on my side
listening to me, believing me, comforting me

the darkness has disappeared from the scar
which has turned into a fine, light line

and darkness has lifted from my life

would you have held me?

I wanted out of your cold, dark house of silence
filled with lies and denial
where understanding and compassion did not live

the man I was engaged to was not right for me
but I drowned in anxiety and had no contact with my Self

why did you not suggest therapy for your eighteen-year-old child
filled with anxiety—who could not sleep?
how could you allow me to be numbed and silenced
with Librium and strong sleeping pills?

what would you have said and done had I told you
I am confused and upset
because I was raped by my father when I was sixteen
it tore my mind apart
I did not want to hurt you
I have been too afraid to tell you

I have wanted to get out of here for a long time
        and marriage seems the only way out
I am afraid I cannot make it on my own
        I have no self-confidence—separations terrify me

I see this man as my only way out—but I cannot connect with him
emotionally, mentally, physically or spiritually

would you have held and comforted me, mother
would you have told me
how awful that this crime happened to you
I am so sad that you had no one you could talk to
that you were plunged into an abyss of despair and confusion
that you could not trust me to listen to you and believe you

help you and protect you
even if it meant that I had to leave my marriage

———————————

when I finally had the courage to tell you the truth
I did not hear
I am terribly sorry how you suffered
that you needed years of therapy to deal with this trauma
I am sorry that you were afraid of me
and that I could not be there for you all these years
but I am here for you now—I want to make a difference
I want to be a different mother

no, I did not hear these words

see—I told you so

in your presence I never dared
to talk honestly about me and my life
but once when I was a young woman—married only a few years
I told you that I married so young
because I wanted to get out of the house

never will I forget how you looked at me
if looks could kill
your eyes would have killed me right then and there

you tolerated only the glorious vision of the perfect family
you silenced the truth for it
without hesitation and remorse, again and again

problems and illness did not bring out motherly comfort in you
instead words hit me like a whip
see—I told you so
pull yourself together
who do you think you are!
what a bad girl you are!
are you crazy?
you are hysterical—just imagining things

your uncaring cruelty ripped across my soul
made me feel abandoned and wrong

my pain and problems
turned into insurmountable catastrophes
and left me behind defeated
a failure

one-way street to pity

my pain and needs, my problems and worries could not exist
our relationship was about nothing but you, mother
I could not tell you of my despair—you did not wish to hear it

like a stuck record turning around and around
in the same hopeless cycle
our relationship was consumed by your needs
while my needs were considered impertinence and impudence
and my problems were whipped away

your arms never held me—you did not comfort me
your words and actions did not try to understand and support me
your biting judgments and blame destroyed my self-confidence
pushed me deep into inconceivable loneliness
with no one on my side—but you expected and demanded that
I be unconditionally at and on **your** side—always

trained to feel endless pity for you I felt sorry only for you
never for myself—all compassion went towards you
a woman consumed by endless self-pity
I tried my best to understand and excuse you—I worked hard
to not be a problem for you, to not need your support and help

our relationship was filled with your suffering
—mine had no value—no right to exist, be heard and changed

in this reversal of the mother-daughter relationship
there was no room for my plight
for what I needed to talk about—you refused to hear it
you wanted me to lie—and you still demand that I lie for you

the truth could and cannot be alive between us
our relationship ended in silence

fallen out of grace

written in Mexico, 2003

baby—fallen out of grace
for nine months you were nursed and held by your mother
had looked into your mother's eyes
how safe and secure you felt during these precious moments
how loved you felt in your mother's arms

although fed according to a strict schedule—at least
your hunger for human contact was stilled a few times every day
while you felt comforted and at home in your mother's arms
but after nine months the breast-feeding ended
your mother got up—she had more important things to do now
than to hold a baby—she was six months pregnant
a new baby would arrive soon

you, her firstborn baby, fell from your mother's lap
—dumped, fallen-out-of-favor load—left behind on the ground
you never found comfort in your mother's arms again

you struggled so hard to fulfill her expectations—but it was never
enough—your mother kicked you, the lump on the floor
with criticism and harsh words—with beatings and punishments

as more and more children were born
the eldest was pushed farther and farther aside
had to become more and more "reasonable" and "modest"

the baby, fallen out of grace, screams—*why am I here?*
why can I not be in your arms again?
what is wrong with me that you don't hold, don't love me
that you don't care about me, my tears, my pain, my screams?
why don't you see me—abandoned, lonely, suffering?
I love you—I want to be with you

126

13
seeking connection

beggar child

I need to belong somewhere
my hearts wants to be with you all the time
I want to be a part of you—always
I need to feel important to you so that I can have meaning
and live

I am standing in front of your door—a beggar
I study your face to decipher its expression
are you smiling at me?
do you love me?

again and again the beggar comes to the door
desperately asking for the smile
for a tiny token of love

if the beggar gets a penny she walks away
only to return
to try again the humiliating game

the child's need for loving attention is vital, essential
and endless

poor man, rich man—begging for money
powerless child, powerful grownup—begging for love

three hugs

I cannot remember that my mother hugged me
in her presence my body filled with fear—became paralyzed
I did not like how she smelled—somehow morbid as if dead
stiffly we kissed each other on our cheeks to say hello
keeping a distinct and formal distance
I remember the same distant hello and goodbye formality
with my father too when he—a very tall man
bent down to lend his cheek to be kissed

I know that Hotto allowed closeness and hugged me
and there are three hugs with my father that I do remember
the first happened after my car accident
when my father came and took me into his arms—without blame
simply holding and protecting me—I cry thinking about it

at my first wedding he sang poems he had written for me
while he showed slides of photos of my childhood
he started to cry, then I cried too—and we embraced each other

the third one I remember happened when I made an attempt
shortly before my return to Germany
to talk more openly and honestly with my parents about myself
my mother got increasingly hostile and attacked me
while he said—*but, darling*
the child only needs to talk and get it off her chest
whereupon I began to cry and my father hugged and held me
while my mother left the room

when I left their house I started to cry
and cried through the night
suicidal thoughts tormented me as I realized
that I would never have
an open and honest relationship with my parents

without answer

almost thirty years old I told my father
how much I had enjoyed making music with him
his response was
but you could not sing as well as your aunt Mausi

———————

after I gave up studying music my mother told me
that I would have made a good accompanist
were you ever aware how deeply my childhood was marked
by being my parents' good accompanist
while I struggled alone through chaos and darkness?

———————

my brother gave an interview I did with Alice Miller
—published in the German *Psychology Today*—
to my parents—their answer was silence
months later I dared to ask my father if he had read it
his answer was—*you cannot have made this*
you don't know that much about "it"

a friend asked me—*why did he say that?*
I had not thought about it
but knew the answer spontaneously—*envy, it was envy*
he has written a lot—but has never been published

———————

thirty-three years old, I held my mother in my arms and told her
I love you—she did not hug me—she sat next to me like a stone
a tear emerged from her eye as she reproachfully accused me
I will never forgive you for abandoning me
when I needed you the most

I have no clue what she referred to

was it that I had entered therapy
became concerned with my Self and the tragedy of my life
and I was not the perfect eldest anymore?

———————

I had written an essay, "Facing a Wall of Silence"
about how I discovered in therapy
and through taking a class called "Encountering the Holocaust"
part of my family's past
and what that had meant for me and my life

it was published by Allan and Naomi Berger
in their book *Second Generation Voices*

I translated it into German for my mother
she wanted to read it
her answer was
silence

it's all over

his letters are my most precious possession—I hide them
carefully—way back in a long and narrow drawer of my desk
I read them secretly—I know I have to hide this love

but one day I come home from school
to find Jan's letters lying where they do not belong
on my nightstand next to my bed
anxiety rushes into my cells and floods my body
irrational hope calms me—*maybe our cleaning lady found them*

then my mother asks me to come to her room
she wants to talk to me—now I know who found the letters

I can barely walk as I enter her room
my legs feel heavy like lead—as if they cannot carry me in there
the old, well-known terror seizes me—my blood freezes
I feel paralyzed and as if I am about to faint

I leave my mind and my Self outside her door
—as I left them outside the ship cabin too—
the tin soldier enters and deals with this problem
I forgot her lecture but remember
that I had to write Jan a letter to tell him
that "it" was all over—I wrote the letter the same day

that Christmas my father gave me a book
it was a play about the trial against a man named Oppenheimer
called the "father of the atomic bomb," which he helped develop
my father had written a quote in the front of the book
these days we scientists have stepped to the edge of an abyss
we have discovered sin

I gather all the courage I have and walk up to my father to ask

why did you write this?—his answer is—*you know*
I gather even more courage and dare to ask again
why did you write this?
this time he says—*what you experienced this summer is sin*
I walk away silently—yet in his eyes
I saw a strangely different attitude—one of joy and excitement
that I then read as approval

never was another word spoken about Jan
between my parents and me—what did they imagine happened
between a fourteen-year-old teenager
and a twenty-eight-year-old man
during the two short weeks I spent on the island that summer?

he kissed me a few times and hugged me
held me in his arms—is that a sin?

a year later, back at the beach, I meet Jan again
he asks me—*out of sight, out of mind*?
my mouth is sealed—I cannot tell him what happened
I am programmed to such loyalty that I must betray
the most loving, alive, joyful relationship I have known

I see him again when I am engaged
he wonders why I marry so young
you have so much talent—what a shame if you don't develop it

once more we meet years later on the island
he invites me to his parents' new home in the dunes
he is divorced and has a young son
he is surprised that I love life in the United States

how happy I have been when we meet in my dreams

abyss

three times I lost the ground under my feet
three times I tumbled into the abyss of betrayal
with nothing to hold onto
deeper and deeper the fall into a bottomless depth

my mother's murderous attack and her violent rage
scare me to death, shatter my trust in life, render me powerless
I am disabled by fear from the beginning

abandoned by my beloved nanny
my soul is tormented by feelings
of worthlessness
of loneliness

robbed by incest
of stepping into womanhood and a life of my own
my father's betrayal delivers my self-confidence a final blow

three times the earth opened under me—love and trust shattered

I lived like a shadow of myself
tried to please even more desperately to regain a sense of worth
it was the only way I knew how to feel good about myself

love and trust—replaced by fear and submission—
became nightmares

September 11 brings back these feelings of falling into the abyss
the despair and the doubts
how can life go on—how will I live from now on
in a world gone up in flames ignited by hatred

I see people falling, burning—the towers collapsing

in the newspaper I meet the faces and fates of the victims
where is the ground under my feet?
again, I fall
how can I trust life and the world where such madness happens?

I embrace the betrayed child with compassionate understanding
I hold her tragic fate

thus empowered to return to the present with open eyes
I can see now

life and **my** life
reveal their precious, unique nature

I emerge with my quest clearer
my values sharper in focus
my goals and priorities redefined
my journey on a changed course

I must break the silence
I must express my truth
my screams
my book
and my Self
shall live

I thought you would be my friend

after eighteen months I come for my last therapy session
before I must return to Germany
we have never discussed what happens when therapy ends

we will talk to each other when we meet each other in the street
I feel as if the ground opens below me when he says these words
I am in shock, feel betrayed, cannot talk anymore
I just want to get out of his office and never come back
he asks—*something happened—what happened?*
I manage to utter—*I thought you would be my friend*

that day I experienced for the first time in my life
what it feels like to be betrayed—as I cried for hours
I sensed that something terrible had happened with my father
which overwhelmed me with horrible feelings of shame
—long before I remembered the incest

it took my mind many years to recognize the betrayals
that the child had suffered—they overwhelmed me
with unbearable pain, which the child never could have survived
and never could have come to terms with

———————

I trusted and loved you, Hotto, like a mother
I believed that you loved me and cared about me
I believed I was important to you

but you left and did not come back to see me
with you it was like being with a therapist
when the pay stopped—the relationship ended
I thought you would be my friend

———————

Vatti—I trusted and loved you unconditionally
you were my role model—I treasured your love of life
I felt close to you and believed I mattered to you
but on the Queen Mary love and trust ended
I thought you would be my friend

———————————

you loved books, writers and stimulating intellects, Mutti

convinced that my mind and thinking mattered to you
I thought you would be excited about my changes
I was sure that you would welcome my liberation and my writing
but you turned against me and abandoned me

without you at my side
a life mission I saw as enlightening and important
seemed like a petty personal vendetta fueled by revenge
again I stopped writing and having a voice
afraid to be seen as a monster who cannot forgive
and who wants to hurt her mother

it took another twenty years
before I could trust my Self and my voice
value my life and my creativity
and appreciate my uniqueness

with your support
my voice and my book would have lived long, long ago
your support would have given them remarkable, unique power
I thought you would be my friend

14
abandoned

your hand

written in Germany, 1988

give me your hand
I want to hold it
press it against me
I want your hand to feel my tears
and my boundless longing

I want to hold onto your hand
I need to be held
connected

I want to belong to you
I must feel at home

I need a bond from me to you
my origin
my bridge to life
my lifeline of hope

your hand—the last and only holding
at the edge of the abyss
before the fall into nothingness

but you withdrew your hand
I could not hold your hand

desperately stretched out
my hand
went down with me

the bride

I was eighteen, engaged to be married for three months
when anxiety seized me
it took my sleep as I obsessed over what would happen to me
after I died—desperately I read the bible
and any book on death and dying I could find

two weeks into this ordeal I went to see our doctor
tranquilizers and strong sleeping pills were prescribed
he told me that all would be well once I was married
and that I could drive my car
but should have no more than a glass of wine if I did

when I came home my parents wanted to talk with me
we sat in my mother's room
they had noticed that something was wrong with me
it was my father who spoke—my mother remained silent

I told them of anxiety and sleeplessness—my visit to the doctor
my father told me that he had experienced a similar crisis
when he was engaged to my mother—I felt relieved
because now what I experienced seemed less scary to me
not like an indication that I was going crazy
which I was afraid was happening to me

no one ever mentioned therapy, such a taboo where I come from

my only concern was not to be a problem—so I took the pills
heavily drugged for months I believed myself to be well

on the outside I was a smiling and seemingly happy bride
inside a chaos that had tried to erupt
seethed in the volcano of my body
covered by drugs and denial

the car accident

eighteen and drugged, engaged, confused
I drove my car one day not far from my parents' house
it was getting dark and I came down a hill in a curve
when I suddenly saw
a dark figure coming out from behind several parked cars
and walking straight into the street

he came out of a forest to cross the street
where an old pedestrian walkway was hardly visible anymore
I tried to avoid the man with the dark coat and the dark hat
I pulled the steering wheel to the left as I attempted
to drive around him
he never looked up—he never looked at me
but suddenly he started to run—and ran right into my car

I stamped on my brakes
brought the car to a stop in front of a tree, got out, turned around
and ran back to where the accident had happened
I did not see the man
for one moment I desperately believed—it did not happen
but then I turned around and discovered to my horror
the man lying next to my car

I ran into a house at the side of the street
I rang a doorbell—people opened the door
I screamed out what had happened—the people took me inside

then all I remember is my father coming
he hugs me and holds me in his arms
and I cry and cry and cry while I am writing this
a policeman approaches me to question me
my father says—*you cannot question her now—she is in shock*
clearly I remember all this

from the moment I returned home I have no more memories
except for the third day when my fiancé came to visit me
I still can feel him lying down next to me
holding me while he told me that the old man had died

in therapy the first powerful pain came up
when I felt how unbearably lonely I had been
alone in my room during the days after the car accident
no one came to be with me
lying there I felt like a disastrous failure
like a monster, a leper, an outcast
the showpiece had failed, was abandoned and cast out

some time later the walkway was painted clearly and visibly
a traffic light was erected at the scene of the accident
where pedestrians now push a button to cross the street

in court it was an important issue
where I had hit the man in relation to the pedestrian walkway
but I did not know—and no one else could find out
if it had happened on, or next to, the pedestrian walkway
I felt responsible for his death, no matter where it happened
the fine I had to pay did not ease
my sense of severe guilt and responsibility

my afflicted soul became convinced
that this was the final, devastating confirmation
that something **was** terribly wrong with me
that I **was** wrong and **did** everything wrong

I had my driver's license for one month when it happened
I worried that the drugs and my inexperience caused the accident
I was burdened with even more excruciating guilt by a friend
who told me that it was all my fault
because I had had a little wine with her that afternoon

guilt became a flame of torturing pain inside

false guilt versus true guilt

the big wedding party was cancelled
the wedding was changed into a small dinner
it took place two months after the accident happened
shortly before my parents took me away for a vacation
I remember sometimes sitting in the afternoon
crying for some time—then I would go to bed and sleep

I do not remember talking about the accident with anyone
until in therapy I was one day overwhelmed by strong feelings
which frightened me, so I blocked them out
my therapist asked—*what happened*
and I said—*my car accident came up and I felt as if I would faint*
never will I forget his answer
this is a precious chance for us to do our work
these are gold nuggets in here

I could forgive myself for the accident only thirty-four years later
a similar crisis of someone very close to me brought it up
this time I could comfort the abandoned, lonely eighteen-year-old
writhing in agony and self-condemnation
with my love and compassion

to be responsible for the death of another human being
is a life-changing burden
it made me feel like an outsider to the community of men
it marked my life profoundly
it strengthened powerfully my quest and determination
to work in therapy—to conquer my anxiety
and to never be at the mercy of drugs again

I have thought at times that I was capable
of recognizing and leaving behind false guilt, inculcated into me
because of true guilt I incurred

not alone anymore

loneliness erupted as the first painful memory
early in my therapy work
dormant for years—it had been waiting
under the surface of the smiling façade
to emerge

in therapy I remembered those days after the accident
without comfort from my family
numbed by drugs, silence and isolation

I could not cry or experience my emotions
without the support of a compassionate witness
for whom my suffering was real and true

I could not feel such pain on my own
and survive the overwhelming self-blame and self-doubt

after I experienced this loneliness I told my therapist
until now my life has seemed
as if I have been standing in front of a painting
with everyone in my family telling me
it is red—it is beautiful—your family life was wonderful

but to me this painting has always looked black and grim

now that you have looked at it with me
and confirmed that it is indeed black and grim
I know that my perceptions are true
and I do not feel alone anymore

———————

for my next session I brought him a bouquet of colorful flowers

the betrayal of guilt

no more guilt, mother, no more—enough is enough
the curse of guilt poisoned my soul and my life
the weight of guilt has bent and twisted me
I carried it way too long
I hand back to you the biggest lie I was fed

how your verdict of my guilt haunted me
and made me a frightened, silent, submissive coward
who believed—*I am wrong and I do everything wrong*

I believed you that I was innately guilty—to the point
when every feeling, thought, question and need of my own
drowned me in fear—cornered my mind in hopelessness
flooded my body with anxiety

problems meant nothing but an onslaught of guilt
with no one on my side—with my mother always against me

no more guilt, mother, no more—enough is enough
I believed you—how guilty I felt for all the children you had
and whom you experienced as a dreadful trial
I felt responsible for your resentment of it
I felt responsible for you and for easing a fate you resented

I felt guilty for having been born, for existing and for having needs
I believed I was nothing but a problem and burden
but no longer, mother

every step I took away from you, every dream I ever had
every goal that was important to me
any sign of life within me, any longing for love or compassion
only increased the amount of guilt I carried

one day I realized that someone was responsible
but it was not me—I did not bring all these children into the world
how can I be responsible for the lives, decisions and actions
of my parents?

it was a crucial turning point

as I felt betrayed and exploded with painful rage
I returned the responsibility to where it belonged—to you
it never should have rested on my shoulders
the number of children my parents had was beyond my control

the sad truth was—you never wanted all these children
all the help and nurses and money you had
did not change your anger and bitterness over your life

you envied me for the affection others had for me
for the love that came towards me
you burdened me with guilt because of my nature, my radiance
and for the richness of my talents
but no more guilt, mother, no more—enough is enough

you abused my trust and dependence to teach me lies
to burden me with the responsibility for your unhappiness
but no longer, mother

I could not work for my dreams and goals
I could not be on my side because you never were

it was a liberating surprise
to see the truth, to drop the guilt
to become aware of the reality of our relationship
to wear the empowering gown of freedom
and to celebrate the heavenly joy of feeling unburdened

enough is enough—this guilt you implanted into me is untrue
what would my life have been like without it

15
losing my mind

why do I have to believe so much

why do I have to believe?
why do I have to believe so much?
why is believing so important to you?

why must I believe my parents
even if they don't tell the truth?

why do I have to believe that my parents are good and mean well
        although they frighten and hurt me unimaginably?
why do I have to believe that I am a fortunate, privileged child
        when I am terrified and lonely and no one comforts me?
why do I have to believe that problems exist only
        because of my sinfulness and guilt
        while everyone higher in the hierarchy is infallible?

why may I not trust **my** observations, **my** feelings, **my** thoughts?
why are they put down as imagination, hysterical, over-sensitive
attacked as contradiction and disobedience
destroyed as presumptuous, dangerous, rebellious?

why must I believe that it is wrong to trust my Self?
why must I believe in God whom I cannot see?
why do I have to believe that my religion is superior?

why do I have to believe that Jews are bad, a lost people
condemned by God, source of all evil, blamed for killing Jesus?
it was in fact Roman tyranny and the ruthless despot Pilate
that murdered not just Jesus
but uncounted unwanted opponents
on the cross

why do I have to believe that only the "right" belief
grants me God's acceptance and approval?

why does my religion indoctrinate me
with intolerance and inhumanity
anti-semitism and hatred?

only human beings can invent a God
who would condone such arrogance
or insist on such an exclusive, dangerous belief

why do I have to believe that only a belief grants salvation?

was my mind given to me to turn off and believe blindly
or to make use of
      to think for my Self
          to question and recognize
             to find truth?

———————————

the girl kills the overwhelming questions
for which she has no answer

they explode her brain
they make her feel that she is losing her mind

the unnoticed injury

reprimanded for any step of my own
I struggled through fear, persecution, betrayal
but no one recognized how wounded I was—that terrible things
had happened to my brain and emotional health
that intellectual bruises and emotional bleeding
had turned my life into a fearful ordeal

like a badly sprained ankle that could not heal
my mind remained a severely injured part of my body
that kept me from being my Self
from walking and living freely—with confidence and awareness

it made me a cripple
programmed to conform and submit willingly

the behavioral symptoms of the scared, intimidated child
were considered the impertinence of a disobedient monster

no visible wounds, no blood, no witness—no one called a doctor
no one said—*she suffers—she is in pain and needs help*
so the wounds were not treated and festered

the injuries clogged my mind, blocked my thinking
restricted my freedom and independence
took away my confidence and power

I could not walk into life but held on with stiffened reflexes
to what had made the child look good and feel safe
                              approval
                    obedience
              submission
          enduring suffering with a smile
forgiveness

the manic-depressive see-saw

*"as punishment we had to stand in corners,
even next to the garbage cans"*
my sister

any true utterances and spontaneous actions
turned out to be such bad mistakes
with such horrendous consequences
that nothing was left of the child but a disfigured, hopeless corpse
crumpled next to the garbage can

the living corpse is tired of life
writhing with pain, she has sunk to the floor next to the garbage
she feels inadequate—so incapable of doing anything right
she feels like worthless garbage and asks herself
why was I ever born?

to counter devastating feelings—to avoid the fall into depression
she mounts a survival strategy, a façade, an outer shell
a beautiful Barbara—perfect in her parents' eyes
her parents' pride

she gives honor and glory to her parents and her family
she shines for them and lets herself be shown off

the more praise and attention she can gain
the more she finds herself in a bizarre state of exuberance
she feels high and manic in that admired state
where she feels special and believes that she matters

but this state is like skating on thin ice
falling through is only a matter of time
until her aliveness and her feelings and needs resurface

they threaten to cause the fall
back into anguish and despair

when she succeeds at getting attention and praise
when she feels successful and admired
she floats in her manic state
convinced she can do anything—she believes
to be a perfect child

when she falls, worthlessness devours her
and she feels wrong and useless

this emotional see-saw
—created by her parents' treatment—
becomes a curse which runs her life

the grownup woman is still ruled by it and does nothing else
but look for the expectations of others and try to figure out
how to live up to them, how to fulfill them

if she does not receive what she hopes for
she descends into hopeless self-accusations and self-blame
if she succeeds and shines
she gets high in the state of the over-achiever

forced to find this magic potion like a drug she needs to survive
she becomes an empty, glistening shell
behind which looms
the fall
into the darkness of depression

the judge who also prosecutes

my mouth—washed out with soap—for not telling "the truth"
the degrading ritual took place in my parents' bathroom
where I was dragged, my head bent down, held over the sink
where with soap and force
honesty and openness were rubbed and tortured away

the reality of the child did not count as truth
but was considered an annoying parasite—to be exterminated

the child spent all her energy to survive an eternal insane court
that ruled her home
and conducted perfidious interrogations with her

relentlessly accused, confused and brainwashed
she stood powerless and humiliated
in front of the self-righteous prosecutor-judge
who—in one person and doing everything at the same time—
accused, judged, condemned and sentenced her

no means for the child to see through this devilish game
no one to defend her—no one at, much less **on** her side

with systematic barbarity
the judge found something wrong with her child
then ruled and punished with sadistic joy

the child had to confess to things she had not done
and admit bad thoughts she had not thought

all the evilness that—according to this judge—lived within her
seized the child with such guilt and horror
that her brain turned and turned in a maddening whirl
it grew wilder and wilder

until the child's mind spun out of control
and could not make sense of anything anymore
there was no way out—no escape
nothing to hold onto

the judge was malicious
in front of others her mother would hide who she was
her mother was capable of denying what she had said before
without hesitation, shame or scruple

when her mother claimed not to have spoken
        what the child had clearly heard her say
when her mother so obviously lied
the abyss became a hell of madness into which the child fell
and fell
and fell

no hold—nothing to hold onto

falling into the horrendous betrayal of her mother's lies
the child experienced reality—and then herself
as unreliable and crazy
and lost her mind

requiem for an unlived life

I was taught that blessed are those who carry suffering
because they shall be comforted
no, Barbara, you were not blessed and not comforted
no one cared to notice your injuries or your suffering
so you had to hide them—even from yourself

there was no guidance to help you find ways out
guilt and blame were the masters
and the only answers given to you

when you tried to come alive and be true to yourself
the hidden wound of your injured brain
broke open
caused unbearable anxiety in your body
and locked your mind into an endless dark spin

therapy was never considered—who wants a crazy child?
how does that make the family look?
appearances were all that mattered

if your leg had been broken, you would have gotten help
but no one cared to see the fractures of your brain
cared to witness your damaged psyche and know the reasons
your bad genes, your innate madness, your imagination
your over-sensitivity—they all were blamed for your suffering
but never what your parents did to you, or what they believed

you believed your father was a good man of integrity
incapable of making you suffer, of living a lie for years
such a man could never possibly be your father

your father stigmatized sex before marriage as a crime
you entered the ship full of love and joy of life

158

you left it devastated and broken—a mere shadow of yourself
you did not know anymore who you were

drowning in a whirlpool of panic
you believed you had lost all worth—what had become of you?
which kind of woman? who would ever marry you now?

your brain chose the only way out—to forget

no, blessed are not those who are traumatized and who suffer
they are not being heard or comforted
instead many are eager to diagnose and categorize them
from schizophrenia to paranoia—from neurosis to depression
it is nothing but an attempt to hide and silence the truth

if we cannot conceal our broken brains well enough
if we become overwhelmed by unbearable symptoms
we are declared crazy, defective creatures
should we remember and dare to talk about what was done to us
we are condemned as unforgiving
—and thus rendered guilty all over again

we may not scream out our outrage over atrocious crimes

no, Barbara, you could never use your mind like a healthy person
to get an education, build a profession
a loving marriage and family as you dreamed
your mind was too busy concealing the fracture of your brain
controlling the chaos that threatened to shut it down
avoiding crashes into the devouring abyss

you were robbed, in monstrous ways, of life's treasures

even when a man truly loved and desired you
and you dared in your forties to open yourself towards love
your joy succumbed to anxiety and anguish
as falling in love turned into a courageous battle
to confront love betrayed

your parents silenced your voice, your thoughts and your truth
filled your soul with terror, extinguished your integrity and spirit
numbed your intellectual independence

I sing a requiem for you, Barbara
for a life that you could not make come true
for the families and relationships you lost
for the unbearable loneliness of your journey

I sing a requiem for the silences imposed upon you
for your hopeless isolation and loneliness, with no way out
I sing a requiem to express your grief and sorrow
which no one ever recognized and comforted

my requiem will become your song of liberation
for your departure into the truth
I take your hand, you sixteen-year-old, bright, talented teenager
so unfathomably betrayed
I take your hand
I scream out together with you your terribly justified pain
your most understandable outrage—so that they may finally live
I lend support to your hand so that it can express
through writing
your thoughts and feelings

I deliver you out of the abyss of silence, isolation and loneliness
in which you were abandoned and lost

I take your hand—and singing together we leave the darkness
we break the silence—we walk into life—we speak the truth

you are saved
your life begins—although too late for many things—yet in time
to cherish your unique mind and essence
to make your imprint on life

I am at your side
to help you make visible the unforgettable trace of your life

16
worthless

swamp of worthlessness

I see a child stuck in a swamp of messages
that scream her worthlessness

insults and devastating words ooze over her
and cover her like mud
suffocating, she struggles for each strangled breath
desperately she wants to prove her worth
and gain any sign of approval
I am good—I am obedient—I deserve your love
her soul cries

I hear her muffled cries and reach out to her
she grabs my hand—I pull her out
we stand there looking back
a final curse is thrown at us
we hear the words—*unforgiving, ungrateful*

we are daring to flee those who believe the swamp should exist

hearing their accusations and reproaches, my spirit says
take this child forever from this place
where her voice is stifled and her cries are drowned

we turn toward the sun and walk on firm ground into the light
and I know exactly why some people lose their sanity
they cannot escape from the mire of guilt and blame

I have saved this tortured child
I carry her in my arms
I reveal the truth to her

to the swamp we shall never return

shadows

dark shadows cover my life—unaware of them
I consider myself a well-functioning person
and very lucky—with wealthy parents and a wealthy husband

the shadows speak up—anxiety spreads out
shuts down the well-behaved person, robs her sleep at night
closes her mouth when she needs to speak up
blocks her joy of interacting with others
destroys her ability to perform as a pianist

anxiety casts a paralyzing shadow over her life

she decides to give up tranquilizers and blindness
she is determined to ignore all the reasons
one should not do therapy—she wants answers

anxiety conceals dark experiences
suppressed for her survival in her family

anxiety hides the screams of a woman
who clings to beliefs—that she has nothing to complain about
how privileged she is—how spoiled if she is not grateful

but wealth separates and isolates her
like a prison sentence that she wants to, but cannot, escape

barred behind huge walls children—surrounded by wealth—
were made to feel worthless
while a powerful unspoken message was ingrained into them
prove your worth by acquiring wealth—or marrying rich

a son is a god

written in Germany, 1988

I was born as one of the attempts on the path to a son
how worthless I felt after my brother was born
I believed that something must be wrong with me
because I did not have dangling between my legs
this most important and treasured thing
that turned my brother into my father's and grandfather's god
that gave him attention and power I could not even dream of
that granted him rights inaccessible to me

hidden deep inside lived passionate rage at this "small difference"
at this insane injustice that banned the women of my background
from acting freely and from embracing professions

powerless, degraded, desperate, full of hatred
the child's soul burnt her precious life force—while she learned
to succumb to being a member of the lower caste

you had a special wooden door on the island, father
where only the names of the male members of your family
were carved—as if a woman never had crossed this threshold
as if the existence of female family members was insignificant

I tried hard to be wild and tough like a boy
how much I wanted to be a boy
I played soccer with boys, fell often, had countless bloody knees
but nothing worked—my lack rendered me worthless

this special thing gave money and power, influence and status
bigger cars and more rights, university degrees and professions
the freedom of traveling and getting away
and above all the right to rule in a powerful authoritarian way
over the whole family

worthless

Hotto, my dearest nanny, what does love mean to you?
why did you not come back to see me?
we lived together like mother and daughter for years
left behind the child screams—*why don't I matter to you?*
why aren't I important to you? I love you—don't you love me too?
and concludes—*my life does not make a difference*
something is wrong with me—I am worthless

———————————

mother, why do you only find fault with me?
why do you always find something wrong with me?
too loud, too happy, too sad, too inquisitive, too impudent
too difficult, too selfish, too dumb, too disobedient
too this and too that—too straightforward—too exuberant
you handed me over to nurses—abandoned me for months
screamed at me like a fire-breathing dragon—and you beat me
how can I convince you that I am not innately evil
but a worthwhile human being?

———————————

father, what worth and value has my life for you
for a man who despises women with unimaginable contempt?
in your mind I belong to a lower caste
why is for you a woman only defined as an object of sex?
what about actions—working—thinking—writing?
I am your child—powerless at the mercy of your brainwashing
see me, father—I am a human being with a brain and talents too

———————————

the child could not overcome the stain of worthlessness
no matter how hard she tried to prove
her worth to those around her

17
who is my father?

what did you do in the war?

I remember photos of my father—in uniform
next to war comrades
some worked for him after the war—loyally devoted to him

at home he kept a motorcycle and on the coast a boat
he was always ready to leave—"should the Russians come"
he bought refuges for himself in Canada and Argentina
I could never even think the question
why might you have to run?
why would the Russians come for you?
I believed all fathers had motorcycles
and had to escape the Russians—the child thought nothing of it

for my final German school exam I chose to write about a poem
by my favorite poet Ingeborg Bachman
I had enjoyed writing interpretations of her poems before
the poem in the exam was about the war
I struggled for hours—in the end I knew that I had failed
I left crying because I was unable to work with the poem

I had no clue why—what our fathers had done in the war
was not a subject in school or at home
we did not discuss our fathers and what they did in the war

once I started therapy this time came up with such a vengeance
that I realized what dangerous blind spots I had in my past
and how my father's experiences in Hitler's army
were covered by silence

at the end of his life my father was a bent man, broken in spirit
his past caught up with him
after a year in a mental hospital he came home
sat brooding in silence and disappeared into mental darkness

who is my father?

during the first eighteen months of therapy in the early eighties
my therapist looked for research about where I came from
then he found nothing about my generation—the children
of the perpetrators of mankind's most unspeakable crimes

then the war passed
though its consequences were still buried under silence

only a few months into therapy I spent an awful sleepless night
with the devastating feeling that my father
—a German soldier in Russia for three years—
was involved in crimes against Jews
either as a witness or participant

although I could not bear these feelings and thoughts
my body and mind clearly expressed overwhelmingly
their inconceivable message—and I had to listen

I came to my next therapy session in horror and for the first time
my conscious mind dared to form the question
what did you do in the war, father? can I be proud of you?

my father's actions during the war were taboo
the child faced an insurmountable wall—without realizing it
when the family conversation neared the subject of the war
my mother announced in her authoritarian, inimitable way
the war experiences of your father were harmless
this statement meant the end of such a conversation

abandoned in the dark, the child's mind despairs
split into polarized judgments

she clings to good experiences with her father

as proof of his goodness—but senses at the same time
that something is terribly wrong
what kind of man are you, father? have you done evil things?

if her father had committed crimes against humanity—
how could the child ever come to terms with a truth
that would shatter the foundations of her existence?

it was the **not knowing**
that confused her with uncertainty and fear
eradicated her trust in herself, her perceptions, her judgment

when the grownup woman experienced love
this child came forth tormented by the question
who are you, father? are you a good or an evil person?
can I trust you?—but there was no answer
she closed her eyes to discrepancies and lies around her

the grownup woman could not trust
and avoided—love
she did not breathe moral clarity—could not find it around her
her conscience was not allowed to develop and form

I struggled for years—terrified that people I trusted lied to me
I was rendered incapable
of asking questions that would bring me answers
of facing the truth and seeing and judging people realistically
above all—my parents

during a difficult life crisis, the child voiced her agony
as I cried and cried she revealed how her mind
was lost in the dark where she screamed endlessly
father, my beloved father, who are you?

but the walls of the dark room
only returned the echo of her own screams
she went insane in that hopeless darkness
there was no light

arrogance

once I asked my father what war was like
horrible—he replied—*the worst was to be responsible*
for the life and death of other human beings
I also asked what it was like to have served a monster like Hitler
he said—*it was so devastating—you can never imagine it*

a good friend of my father, who lives in a foreign country, told me
of his many conversations with my father deep into the night
but he could not get my father to talk about the war
this man was sure—*your father was hiding what he did in the war*

what did my father—the soldier—think and feel?
what did he do? what was his role?
with what feelings and thoughts did he enter the army
that killed willingly for Hitler's Nazi Germany?

this army was responsible for ending millions
of so-called "worthless lives"
in that insane world anyone but a "strong" man was
worthless
decreasing in rank, from women to the enemies abroad
to the "worthless" peoples in the east
to more and more "worthless" groups of human beings
called "Untermenschen"
all the way down to the absolute most "worthless" group—Jews

fanatic hatred permitted and encouraged fanatic beliefs
widespread religious teachings blamed the Jews
as the infidels and murderers of Jesus
old, pent-up hatred could attach itself to a religious ideology
that had everyone's approval

this army never rebelled
against being turned into killing machines
it preferred to serve monsters and criminals
to blindly murder and exterminate
to spread death like a plague
never questioning those in power, those above in the hierarchy

in this system you bent in submission
to those more powerful, or richer, with more rank or status
and trampled with repulsive arrogance
upon what you considered lower—"down there"

soaked with immoral inhumanity
this system entitled latent sadistic monsters
buried inside inconspicuous, seemingly normal people
to come out and run free
to live out any barbaric monstrosity they could think of
and do this without conscience, without scruples
backed by the authorities

in that hell men felt entitled to humiliate, deride and shame
manipulate, use, control, tyrannize, mistreat, abuse, torture
murder and exterminate
with unimaginable arrogance
anyone they deemed
of lesser worth
or worthless

my father was a perpetrator of that hell
it has cast a dark shadow on my soul and my life

betrayed

I trusted you unconditionally
I believed in you, believed that you meant well
believed what you told me—that you had my best interest at heart

but now I must recognize reality, bewildered
beside myself from grief I awaken to the truth
I am thrown into shock—you never meant what you said
your intentions were boundlessly selfish, abusive, destructive

I must see what I cannot bear to see—you don't care about me
my best interest does not matter to you
instead you took advantage of me
exploited my dependency, my fear, my trust

I feel my brain shattered, my mind thrown into an abyss of horror
my mind cannot handle the reality of your betrayal
has no tool to comprehend your indifference

you were only interested in what served your purposes
and what you could get out of me
I cannot believe that you used me for your sick needs
and sacrificed me for your insane beliefs about life

how unimaginably you took advantage of me
as if I was nothing but a whore
the cheapest one available—you did not even have to pay me

I am screaming and crying from unbearable pain
you have betrayed me—you, the treasured father
to whom I owe my sense of feeling alive and of being my Self
who helped me survive a cruel mother

I was run by the child who idealized you
she ruled over me and ran my being in the world
my relationship with my father was wonderful—she told everyone
because we made music together

deep down, though, I had
ended
my connection with you
my unconscious knew
how I had been betrayed to the depth of my being

my mind bursts recognizing that you were capable
of using my trust with a complete lack of conscience
that you unscrupulously led me
into a darkness
out of which I did not find a way out for thirty-seven years

my tears flood the room where I am crying
uncontrollably
unstoppably
for days

at first I feel as if I am drowning in their stream

as my tears reveal the truth of your betrayal
they communicate the reality of your crime

in the end, these tears carry me away from you forever

out of the darkness I float into truth, freedom and life

a man with charm

father enchanting, magical
home was transformed when he was around
my mother was careful and watched what she did
I felt safer—not afraid of her
my father enjoyed life—my mother was bitter and angry
how the great seducer drew me in and made me adore him
how he charmed me—and he was aware of that
his charisma seduced many around him

but later when I reached out I found no center, nothing real
this manipulator and exploiter had no integrity, no truth

he abused my love and trust to suck me deep into his evil center
into a nightmare of confusion and terror
into an abyss that my mind could not escape by itself
so I denied and repressed what happened

at the edge of that abyss I look down one more time
I hand back to my father his seductive energy
that clouded my vision and shut down my mind
here, father, take it back—it is yours—I return it to you
I don't want it anymore
this is your energy, father—I don't want it anymore
this is your energy, father—I don't want it anymore

as I look ahead I welcome honesty into my life
and I walk away
I never look back again
I cut my ties with him
without you, father, I have gained the clarity to face the truth
found the strength to claim my life
and gained the wisdom to embrace the values I longed for

Ritzka

I was visiting Germany the year before my father died
my brother asked me to see him one more time
he felt it was important—so I came
the incest still kept from my consciousness

I was told that my father spent his days in bed
with his eyes closed
without contact with the people around him
in mental darkness
I expected to just witness for awhile a corpse
waiting between life and death to die

but my father opened his eyes and clearly recognized me
while I cried and said over and over again
I am so glad to see you

he responded to me—he clearly knew who I was
I told him I had married an American pilot and he said "*wow*"
he wanted to see pictures of him
so I ran to my car and got them
he wanted me to play the piano for him—and I did

before I left I asked him to say the special name
only my father had used for me

with his toothless mouth he gave me a big smile
and said—*Ritzka*
and I asked him—*say it again*
and he said one more time with this amazing smile—*Ritzka*

it was my last encounter with my father

three monkeys

three monkeys stood on your desk, father, facing you
and three more monkeys stood on the music cabinet
next to your desk—looking at you

the first monkey covered with his hands his mouth
the second his eyes and the third his ears
one keeps his mouth shut—the other does not wish to see
and the third one does not wish to hear

you lived like this, father, silent, blind and deaf
creeping through life like a coward
without honesty and openness
you followed the authority of your father and other father figures
as if they were gods
but you could be a master of arrogant condescension
toward those with less status and power
people I knew were intimidated when you answered the phone
in your brisk way—and they hung up

you did not know how to honor life
you closed your eyes and ears—you kept your mouth shut
you took your silence with you to your grave

in the house with the three monkeys
independent thinking, awareness and the truth
were unwanted—and persecuted like crimes

I leave your convictions behind me, father
I claim the power of my very own eyes and ears
of my senses and talents—and of my very own voice

18
I wanted to be a writer

contradiction

I wanted to be a writer—but where I came from
a thinking human being with her own thoughts and feelings
was not wanted

thoughts, feelings, needs of my own
that dissented from ruling opinion
were stigmatized by my mother as the sin of contradiction
mercilessly persecuted—eliminated by severe punishment

I became a polite liar, a friendly "yes-man"
who agreed to everything and always understood

a puppet hanging by her parents' strings
telling them what they wanted to hear

if a thought of my own ever made it to my brain
I was trained to murder it

to think independently and to feel freely
—these essential human needs and basic human rights—
were systematically fought and destroyed
as if a great crusade had to be waged—and won
against a most threatening power
against a dangerous enemy
against an evil heretical dissenter

how could a little child be perceived as such a monster?

the crime of having an imagination

I wanted to be a poet—but the obstacles
to becoming a thinking and feeling human being
were unconquerable

until I was fourteen I shared a bedroom with my two sisters
unwanted and burdensome
children were banished into a dark room
shoved away into bed as early as possible
lying there for hours, unable to sleep
we were not allowed to talk or read—no light was allowed

in this dark dungeon my sisters would suggest a word
which I used to make up a story to tell to my sisters
one of my sisters later told me—*your stories helped me survive*
they provided warmth and comfort
but when the crime of talking in the dark
was discovered—we were beaten

stories were not allowed—three silent robots must be raised
no use for a child with imagination who loved to tell stories

when I entered school and could barely write
I asked in a letter to Santa for a pen and a book
—my only wishes that first Christmas I could write—
in school I began to write with joy and great delight
my mother regarded my long essays as exaggerated whims
full of useless fantasy and fancy

eventually I stopped telling stories—instead
I became a passionate reader, interested in the stories of others
but this turned out to be another crime

women can't write

I wanted to be a writer—but to write freely
was to my father the crime of decadence
poems must rhyme and "make sense"—cannot be "too long"

how I loved poems as a teenager
but my father despised and hated what did not fit his prejudices
he also was contemptuous of women who desired
to think for themselves and stand on their own two feet

my father was conceited about his world view
which he had constructed at the age of eighteen
immensely proud that he never had to change it
he repeated it over and over with a god-like self-righteousness
he considered it eternally valid
and kept it in place with stupid arrogance all of his life

my father seemed to me as if balancing on very high stilts
where he and his world view were dangling so precariously
that he felt compelled to systematically destroy
whatever could have shattered this shaky balance

my mother had eliminated contradiction in early childhood
the child's resulting fear and terror kept the command in place
in my teenage years it was my father's turn
to reinforce that command
and to eradicate with equal fanaticism
the mind of a blossoming, bright woman

he spoke down to me with sarcastic derision and mockery
he pointed his finger to his temple to indicate to his daughter
that her thoughts were crazy, not even worth being listened to

with authoritarian zest he established his power and superiority

my father's gestures, words and actions
spoke of an inconceivable, incessant scorn
and such a blind, condescending hatred of women
that I avoided talking with him

the ruler of the family
—as well as the official family philosopher—
did not tolerate contradiction
his opinions had to be accepted, his wishes had to be fulfilled
his commands could not be questioned
but had to be executed
willingly

once or twice I asked him to read verses I loved
only to find angry and judgmental comments
written in his stiff old German Gothic writing style
next to my beloved poems

once or twice I dared to contradict and even yelled back
when he raised his voice
to furiously condemn
the "junk" I was reading

father and daughter ended up screaming at each other
the "degenerate" book flew into the corner
he vowed to visit the teacher
who placed "such trash" in front of his child
I was seventeen

I had forgotten this scene—my sister told me about it

19
without parents

"There was a dimension missing in him, a capacity to feel which his childhood had blotted out, allowing him not to experience love but only romanticized substitutes for love. Pity, compassion, sympathy and empathy were not part of his emotional vocabulary."

Gitta Sereny, *Albert Speer: His Battle with Truth*

Hitler's children

some people believe that with the war's end and Hitler's death
Nazi ideology ended—but deeply imprinted into my parents
it continued its destructive power
it ruled family life—concealed in my parents' minds and souls

my mother, born in 1925, was raised by a strict, cruel mother
who was the daughter of a German governess

deeply formed as an enthusiastic teenager in the Nazi youth
formed by insane beliefs—*tough like leather, hard like Krupp steel*
my mother despised emotions as hysteria
fought illness as hypochondria
and vulnerability as the frivolous fussing of a weakling

my father, born in 1913, learned to follow and obey
first in his family—then as Hitler's soldier
he could not question his authoritarian, sly, patriarchal father
until very late in life
trained to ignore his feelings my father felt emotions
through music, hunting and nature
he despised fear—yet was a fearful, haunted man
he had no courage to face reality and his past—but believed
that by shooting big impressive animals he could prove
how brave and strong he was—but he lived his life as a coward
running away from himself, the truth and life

duty and obedience were eternal law to my parents
dutiful hypocrisy filled their world
the moral air I breathed consisted of silence and dishonesty
of blaming the victim and excusing the perpetrator
where I was meant to have a moral center
I developed a void

lost values

written in 1986

you want to teach me responsibility, values, religion, morals
but I look at your generation and at what you did
—or did not do—when Germany was Nazi Germany

what you want to teach me did not prevent unheard-of crimes

your values, in fact, made them possible—you teach me
—obedience and duty—but they made these crimes possible
—a culture that values most highly the beautiful and aesthetic
       but not truthfulness and speaking up
—a religion that centers on salvation through the right belief
     which means it wants blind followers
     not independent, freely thinking human beings
     who trust and follow their conscience and inner voice
—you treat me with violence, which these crimes spread all over
they became the gruesome trademark of this cultured nation

you teach me a dark double morality
with no room for the pained screams of a human conscience
where people learn to look away and be silent
Shoah would never have happened otherwise

the failure of your values proves to me that they are worthless
you ask me—*where are your new values?*
I don't know yet—all I know is—I cannot live by your values
what you pass on to me has not prevented the ruin of our world
the downfall of your humanity

your values, your religion, your culture, your morality
are worthless to me—they died—they went up
in those flames that burnt millions of human beings
among them one-and-a-half-million children

control

mother and father—controllers of questions about the past
don't ask me—I have worked through everything
but if you have worked through everything—then
you must be able to tell me about it and share it with me
then you can **answer** my questions
explain how you worked through it—and your conclusions

but her parents have the last word
they don't answer questions but erect walls
you did not live then—you may not have an opinion
you simply cannot judge it
but—please—tell me—what were you thinking—then
we don't need your questions—we did our very best
we had no other choice
but—please—tell me—why do I never hear:
it was horrible, I cannot forget, cannot comprehend it
over and over again I have thought about it
our generation carries guilt and an unbearable responsibility
we leave a grave and terrible burden behind for your generation
I found some answers and drew conclusions
I have made changes in my life
I have become engaged in certain causes
because of what happened
because of what I have come to learn
I need to become part of affecting a tiny change
I want to and will do something so that it may happen
never again
never again
never again
you and your generation never said anything like this
your only answer was to drive out my questions
to forbid my thinking, suppress my thoughts, to block my own way

merciless

merciless is the word that comes to my mind
when I think about you
mercilessly you pumped fear into me
persecuted me with accusations and cruel punishments
and tortured me with your hatred, mother

merciless and unforgiving was your judgment of me
merciless were your condemnations and contempt
merciless and unforgiving were your silence and hostility
merciless your indifference and your expectations of me
merciless your demands for subjugation and obedience
merciless your coldness—unforgiving your betrayal of your child
merciless your lies and deception—unbearable your hypocrisy

what mattered to you was—**what will people say**
you once told me how wild you were to have your sixth child
so that people would not say that you had the five others
only to have a boy
but the truth is—you had all these children to have a boy
what a sad reason to bring a child into this world
as a cover up for the truth

merciless was your refusal to listen to me, to understand me
to ever see my side, to respect my integrity, my feelings
my dignity, my humanity, my rights

with you I could not experience
that having a mother can mean protection and compassion
honesty and loyalty, loving support, safety, home

the word "mother" made no sense to me
until I rescued the child from you and mothered her myself

accepting the truth

the first dream in my life and in therapy about my mother ended
while I wondered what to do with my mother—stuffed
in a garbage bag sitting in front of me
I was shocked by that dream—I was a good daughter
she would not have dared to see her relationship with her mother
as a disastrous failure

in my first dream about my father in my life and in therapy
    I come to his funeral—when I look into the casket
    I only see his head and upper torso
    the lower part of his body from the waist down is missing

early on, my unconscious informed me clearly
how our relationship had ended for me
my father died in the year before the incest memory resurfaced
I did not attend his funeral—then I was forty eight years old

I had these dreams about my parents when I was
thirty three years old—but I needed twenty more long years
before I gave up idealizing my father
and trying to reach my mother
early on—in the images and metaphors of these dreams—
my unconscious revealed to me
my truth and the reality of my relationship with my parents
long before I was able to accept and live with them

who inside of me saw so clearly and so early the truth
and told me about it?
who inside of me revealed a reality that filled me with terror
and that I did not consciously know?
who lives there and knows—what it took me years to understand?

how many, many years did it take me to live in truth

escaping

written in Chicago, 1992

forty-two years old, I have moved back to Chicago by myself
I have left my marriage, both children are in college
for the first time in my life I live by myself

one morning as I perceive awakening in my bed
      I watch my cat playing a cruel game with a bird
      catching it—threatening its life
      then letting it go—over and over again

      then the cat climbs on my bed and turns into a man
      who is lying down on me, pressing me down, suffocating me
      I am terrified
      in this moment I feel that the man is real
      and that my life is in danger

as I lie there, afraid for my life, wondering what to do
a long time passes—until I realize—
I am at home
lying safely in my bed
no one is on top of me—no one is with me
I am alone and safe

as I immediately write down what seemed to me
as if it was truly happening, like a hallucination, a waking dream
I realize that the cat is my mother, the bird is me
the cat turns into my first husband
who became an overpowering presence in my life
which almost suffocated me
I have escaped them both

what I wish I had said

written in Mexico, 2004

no, father, no—don't touch me—don't try to seduce me
no, father, no—don't come near me—my first time
goes to a man I have chosen
I want to love with dignity and beauty
not with the stigma and terror of committing a crime

no father, no—leave me alone
I want to consent consciously—I want truthful passion
when another human being enters my body
how dare you take these rights away from me

no, father, no—I don't want to give my virginity to you
don't rob me of my sexual awakening
don't deprive me of sexual fulfillment for years to come

my body is a holy temple that you may not abuse and desecrate
my soul is the divine spark in me
        that you may not toss into turmoil and fear
my mind is my most precious life commodity
        that you may not throw into a dark night of confusion
my Self is life's precious gift
        you may not destroy its power and confidence

no, father, no—I don't want to wake up
night after night, accusing myself
I don't want my brain to go round and round in circles
tormenting itself with hopeless explanations
wondering—*what is wrong with me that this could happen?*

no, father, no—I will do everything to prevent
you taking my sister on the same trip next year
away from home, alone with you, she is vulnerable too

no, father, no—I forbid you to commit the crime of incest
my life has been entrusted to you for protection and guidance
not for reckless exploitation and vile treachery

no, father, no—this is my body—not yours
this is my life—not yours—you don't own me
I have a life I want to live, a sexuality I want to unfold—not bury
I don't owe you my body, my virginity, my life
they are mine and it is up to me to decide what to do with them
I am not your possession but your responsibility
don't you dare use my love for you to blind me
don't you dare abuse the obedience programmed into me
don't you dare numb my defenses through seductive lies
don't you dare touch me in any inappropriate way
don't you dare cross a sacred boundary
        firmly established as powerful law by society

no, father, no—I don't want my soul to drown in guilt and shame
I don't want to plunge into a nightmare of self-blame and fear
I don't want to do years of therapy
in order to be able to climb out of a morass of terrifying self-hate

the scales are falling from my eyes—I am shocked to see
what an irresponsible man and brute you are
fiercely will I guard my Self and my life against you
and not let you near or trust you ever again
I have to walk away from you—to be safe—to have a life
to grow and develop as a human being

it horrifies me to realize
that you are capable of pushing me into the abyss of betrayal
I fell and fell for years
until love enabled me to uncover your crime and your guilt
        empowered me to liberate my Self from guilt and blame
        and hand the responsibility back to you where it belongs
until I found the strength to look you in the eyes and finally say
        no, father, no—don't touch me—don't come near me
        go away—I am better off without you

20
painful layers of silence

unbearable silence

your silence is a black night around me
the annihilation of my existence, of my desire to live
of my love—a burning flame—*look at me, listen to me*
hear me, notice me—I love you

your silence—a dungeon without light that imprisons me
alone in my dungeon the black night devours me
with endless loneliness

my screams and questions—without answer
I cannot live—without answer
I cannot become a human being—without answer

I have grown silent, lost my words
I can only answer your silence with silence, too

I close the door between us
I cannot bear the pain over your indifference, father
so I leave your dungeon of the black night
in order to be with my mother in her world

although I am persecuted and tortured there
I have no other choice—either the black night of your silence
or the hell of her persecution and fear

never could I choose the dungeon of the black night
because hope did not exist there
I would not have survived without hope

painful layers of silence

unexplored silence

at the very beginning of therapy I worked with a psychoanalyst
psychoanalysts can be very quiet while they wait
for "transference" to unfold—but sometimes
I did not feel like talking—when we both were silent
the silence between us troubled and confused me
hurt and enraged me—and became so unbearably painful
—howling inside like a deadly injured animal—
that I wanted to leave his office to never come back—then
I had absolutely no clue what an incredibly powerful role
silence had played in my childhood and throughout my life

---

silently abandoned

Hotto, my nanny, my mother for six years, leaves me
disappears—silently—into silence—the child does not hear
anything anymore from the woman whom she loves and needs

early in therapy I drive my twelve-year-old son to school
he is very quiet that morning—until my pain
over unbearable silences erupts—and I, his mother, cry
and say—with inappropriate despair and uncaring narcissism—
why are you so silent? do you hate me?
my astonished son answers quietly but firmly
I don't hate you, mom
screams, meant for people in our past, tend to erupt
destructively and with a vengeance with our own children
I am no exception—my scream over loosing my beloved Hotto
surfaced not where it originated but with my son

---

reproachful silence

many years ago, twenty-eight years old, I was about to move
to another continent with my first husband and our children
I was on the island visiting my parents to say goodbye
during the last evening before I left, my father played records
Tchaikovsky's music, reminiscing and talking with me
my mother remained silent like a stone, all evening
when I went to bed that night I felt as if a heavy stone inside me
had grown bigger and bigger over the course of the evening
until it had filled and extinguished me with guilt
how indescribably glad was I to get far away the next day

---

banned through silence from the family

a fight breaks out between my family and my first husband
over money—I am betrayed by silence—no one tells me the truth
I am deceived and kept in the dark—by my mother
who does not wish that a marriage should end "over money"
and by a husband whose dark side creates chaos
for years I drown in confusion and pain—caught in-between—
until I decide to leave Germany and return to America

my mother demands that the truth be withheld from me
no chance to decide for myself if I want to end a difficult marriage
where I have suffered for a long time—a marriage that
with my family's support, I might be able to leave
—instead my loyalty becomes the battleground

when I learn the truth, my family's betrayal comes as the
greater shock that hurts unimaginably because their silence
has pushed me into isolation and abandonment
torn apart my loyalty, appeared like blame
and robbed me of my trust, my family, my dignity and honor

trust is the foundation
upon which relationships and love may build

incest—answered with silence

several years of silence have passed between me and my family
when my youngest brother visits me in Chicago to reconnect
my mother never tries—finally I write her to reestablish contact
taking upon myself any blame for years of silence—she answers
and for some time a few letters go back and forth
during this time the incest memory surfaces

our first meeting after many years takes place on the day
before my son's wedding in a hotel—I don't mention incest

it takes a few months to write her a letter
I describe my childhood and tell her about the incest
and express that my intention is not to blame
but to share the truth and create honesty between us
the honesty and openness I need to live

at first she believes me because, as she writes, she knows
that I do not lie and do not want to harm her
I don't dare to think—marred by suspicions—
that for the first time in my life I feel a mother at my side

when I ask her to support me when I tell my brothers and sisters
my suspicions are confirmed—the door that seemed opened
closes—now she accuses me of lying

but I inform my brothers and sisters and receive
a furious letter from my mother
full of judgmental accusations, condemnations
and empty sayings like—*talking is silver, silence is gold*

with all her might she has now slammed the door shut

I meet her one more time at a family function the following year
where my mother wants to speak with me
we talk for a few moments—and she informs me
that I misunderstood her
she does not intend to break off our relationship

I am true to my Self for the first time in my life as I ask her
what kind of relationship can we have if I must deny the truth?

once more her answer is—and remains—silence

the child inside suffers greatly
abandoned by her mother for the very last time
she falls into the abyss of betrayal
     she writhes in agony
         she does not want to say goodbye
            she still clings to her illusions
        she longs for a mother
     she can't let go of her hope to build love with her mother
she believes that
forgiveness
will give her the mother she has always longed for

I hold and comfort her while she screams
for a long time
from excruciating pain
why is my mother not with me—by my side?

carrying her in my arms I walk away
into the freedom of living in truth

the curse of silence

it is cold in my family—an icy wind blows me away
frozen in loneliness and fear, I flee the storm of hostility
cast out, I shiver in the desert of isolation—the family closes
its doors against a monster, banned like a leper
who wants the truth to live—the family sacrifices the child
to serve the gods of good appearances
in whose shadow light cannot shine—the victim
—blown away by a storm of accusations—
drops into the abyss of abandonment

walls of silence serve the perpetrator—they hide a crime
whose consequences are handed down to the victim
as the ultimate punishment

the path to good appearances is paved with graves of victims
buried under shame and guilt—the sermon at their graves says
you are guilty for trusting and loving your fathers
how can they ever communicate what happened to them?
how can they ever tell of their suffering—when the perpetrator
is not held accountable but protected by family and society?
how can they speak their truth with dignity and decency?
fundamentally betrayed, they fall into the black hole of deceit

no one takes care of their graves

the victim—hopelessly alone when the crime is committed—and
when she has to bury the crime under silence for years
when she confronts the truth and dares to break the silence
        —she may do anything—but—not—this—
drowns with the millstone of guilt around her neck
then she is honored with a tombstone which says—*I forgive*

her screams—suffocated forever

21
hopeless

night and day

I used to get upset and anxious
when the sun set and the day ended, when the light left
and the darkness of night began to surround me

I remember how anxiety crept into me and seized me
for the first time—I was eighteen years old
it happened one evening as the sun went down
I was standing in front of my parents' house
saying good night to my fiancé

the anxiety did not leave, did not let me sleep anymore
built to an overwhelming fear with the obsessive thought
what will happen to me after I die?
I was terrified of what awaited me after I died

in therapy I understood that day and night were metaphors
for what my parents symbolized for the small child
light and day represented being—without deadly fear—
in a good world the child believed she shared with her father
father meant connection, closeness, safety, light and life
father meant moments filled with joy and harmony
father meant contact with her Self

darkness and night meant the terror and hopelessness
the child suffered—lost and lonely—in her mother's world
mother meant a cold world of emotional and physical distance
mother meant an unbridgeable abyss, darkness, night, death
mother meant the child losing her center—losing her Self

my soul tried to communicate
you cannot be alive and yourself in this marriage
—but I could not communicate with my soul
and there was no one to teach me how to understand myself

actions

actions of my own free will—actions out of deep convictions
actions without coercion, stemming from my own wishes
I don't know them
everything I do speaks of submission and powerlessness
everything I do screams—*it is all in vain*

imprinted into every cell of my body a curse is my master
no matter what you do—you cannot change your fate

actions out of love—judged as vain groveling
actions out of pride—condemned as impudence
actions from inner strength—banned as shameless presumption
being true to my Self—eradicated as arrogant and self-centered
following my conscience—scorned as a family traitor
—with evil intent

who can live in such madness without loosing her mind?
who am I—if I am not defined by what I do
by my very own actions?
was I not born to be true to my Self?

all I knew were the heavy chains of your beliefs and rules
that tied my hands and feet to you, mother and father
they rendered me incapable of walking and acting freely

actions and steps of my own were greeted with such hatred
that they became impossible

I only knew actions to survive—but not to live

writing is the first true and free action of my life

to write down my thoughts and feelings
marks the turnaround—my departure

as I write
      I revive my feelings and honor them
      I become conscious of my needs and dreams
      I take my observations and conclusions seriously
      I develop the strength to protect my Self
      I discover my wishes and passions
      I form my convictions and values
      I let my conscience speak up and guide me

my true Self emerges
as I write it dares to come out
becomes visible on page after page before my eyes

writing is my path to know my Self
empowering me to become true to my Self

writing initiates actions
as the expression of my true Self

the trap

never may you speak ill of your parents
you can criticize and judge yourself and others—but never
your parents and their actions
because—*they always mean well—you must be grateful to them*
in order to forgive them you must ignore
what they did to you in the past—or do to you in the present
who cares if they don't repent, don't feel remorse
no one wants to know—have they stopped hurting you?
are they willing to look at themselves? have they changed?
you are their child—don't make a fuss—accept abuse and lies
the deeply engraved commandment demands—*honor them*

I lived like that—blind, without dignity and integrity—but full
of self-hatred—incapable of questioning my parents, their actions
incapacitated to recognize and name reality correctly
I sacrificed my perspective and my truth
for a forgiving, benign—and untruthful view of my parents
one that refused to know the facts
that could not question their integrity and motives
that made me follow their beliefs and spoken and unspoken rules
I believed, I obeyed—and felt so guilty for every critical thought
that I drowned it immediately in forgiveness—no, in blindness

I accepted and endured mendacity, lies, inhumanity, betrayal
as irrevocable—they were the essence of my relationships

as I recognize the reality of my relationship with my parents
as I confront the truth with courage—I am isolated and cast out
what seems unbearable at first makes me go my own way
liberated through exile—I discover life

what would our world look like if the fourth commandment said
honor your children?

lonely star

in your presence I did not dare to be honest
once when I was a young woman—married for a few years
I told you that I married so young to get away from home
if eyes could kill—your eyes would have killed me

pain and complaints produced angry, scornful eyes
self-confidence triggered contemptuous derision
questions and tears caused accusations and condemnations
problems and despair brought an onslaught of blame and guilt
joy and spontaneity led to lectures and judgments—my thoughts
my feelings were drowned in damnation and sarcastic ridicule

the child's truthful utterances were met with hatred

abandoned, lonely star—drifting lost and aimlessly
through an endless universe—this is how the child felt
once in school we looked at magnified images of stars
against the black vastness of the universe
and powerful feelings of loneliness overwhelmed me frightfully

when her parents' eyes fell approvingly upon the child
she believed she mattered, was important, her life had value

filled with the illusion of being loved
the child disregarded being careful and watching out
believed for a dangerous moment she was safe

as she betrayed her perceptions and true Self
as she trusted where there was no basis for trust
she was fundamentally deceived

and the little star came unmoored in the firmament

the bird and the wall

written in Germany, 1986

you are a wall in front of me
I throw my timid love and my questioning longing towards you
but they bounce off, fall to the ground, return back to my hands

the wall is hard and cold, tall and invincible
stone by stone built from moral commands and laws
constructed by strict rules of behavior
there is no room for justice or forgiveness, no room for love
the law belongs to you, the wall—it is always on your side

my arms are tired from throwing
my heart fills with endless disappointment
with frustration, pain, even rage and hate
wasted, useless agony—how I can feel with Sisyphus

I am a bird who is learning to fly—tiny, impatient, frightened
excited and impetuous I spread my wings and try—I fly
my companions are love for life, curiosity, fearful apprehension

but again—there is the wall—I bounce against it
numbed, deadened, filled with anxiety
I find myself back on the ground
I make several attempts—but the wall is too high and too strong
for my weak wings, my insecure movements, my inexperience

one day, unnoticed by anyone, I, a battered bird, give up

within the boundaries of the wall I crawl on the ground
crippled—mutilated—my rage petrified—my protest dead
my disappointment fills me with black hatred
timidly I limp and hop on prescribed and ordered tracks
sometimes I look yearningly at the sun—shining beyond the wall

22
hatred—the banned feeling

call it by its true name

hatred against one's own child is not called by its true name
not labeled correctly for what it really is
but excused, justified, hidden behind elaborate concepts

hateful behavior against the child does not go by the name of
hatred—but is labeled as *"for your own good"*
and euphemistically disguised as "education" or "discipline"
but beatings **are** torture—they communicate hatred
humiliating and mocking a child are expressions of hatred
because they hurt and degrade the child and are meant to do so
they imprint the behavior and language of hatred into the child

who punishes parents for their mistakes?
why is punishment only handed out to children who need
parental support and guidance,
orientation, understanding and compassion
to learn the language of love?

this hatred comes cloaked in the robe of virtue, *"I only mean well"*
the child—a dependent, powerless, blind believer—
is taught to regard hate-filled behavior as love
the passion of suffering as unavoidable
and forgiveness as the tool to ignore and deny reality

the child's answer to her parents' hatred towards her
her outrage, protest and pain are condemned
as whiny, unforgiving, revengeful—she may not express them
her need for self-protection and self-love
are ridiculed and judged as the crime of selfishness

old hatred is passed on to children as a good deed
as we allow a destructive tradition to continue
as children are tortured by violence, again and again, on and on

what the language of hatred reveals

the dark night of hatred does not recognize its source
the plight of the humiliated, tortured, helpless child
because hatred towards your own parents is
condemned, denied, covered with silence
buried under the command to honor and forgive them

the source of blind hatred stems from the suppressed outrage
and the unacknowledged pain of the tormented child
it may lash out later, released with political or religious approval
towards others—towards those perceived as a threat
to one's identity, safety, or to one's beliefs

unrecognized and unacknowledged by society
this hatred cannot be overcome
unless it is faced honestly and healed inside
unless its origin is revealed—the passion of the powerless child
the suffering and cross of the persecuted child
whose basic needs for protection, help, safety and love
remained unfulfilled

hatred is outrage that could not be experienced or acknowledged
as inhumanity and hatred were handed down to her
the abused and mistreated child even had to beg for forgiveness

silenced by the law of forgiveness
this outrage is forced deeper and deeper into the child's soul
where it becomes unconscious hatred and never-ending pain
a volcano forms—ready to explode at any time

but hatred—experienced and understood—
reveals the child's nightmare
hatred—accepted and compassionately embraced
—witnessed by a therapist who is on the child's side

tells the truth of the humiliated, abandoned child

the truth reaches her consciousness
as if a lost and sunken ship is finally rescued
brought from the dark, invisible depth of the ocean
to the surface of the water

the truth of an unbearable situation is revealed
the truth of the tortured child

recognized, acknowledged, accepted
the truth is welcome and finally known—and here to stay

no more need to hate oneself or others

understood and compassionately embraced
hatred can be released
its destructive energy
is transformed into an empowering strength
to lovingly take care of my needs
to fulfill my passions
to build a meaningful life

hatred of my parents that became conscious and integrated
painted a clear picture of my childhood reality
and removed me
from my parents' beliefs and destructiveness

empowered to set boundaries—I become my Self

now I know the truth
now I can live in truth and be true to my Self
as I forgive myself for not allowing the truth to live for so long

the language of love

the baby does not understand words
the words—I love you—mean nothing to her
she feels loved when arms hold her
when she feels and smells her mother's body
hears her mother's beloved voice and looks into loving eyes

the baby does not feel loved when pain is inflicted
by holding her up on her legs just as she is born
or when she is separated from her mother
whose body and voice have been her home for nine months
the baby does not feel loved when beatings hit her tender body
when pain and fear destroy her trust in her mother and in life

she is not taught the language of love
but the language of violence and indifference
a behavioral language is already taught to her
when she has no words
when her brain is most vulnerable, growing dramatically
and has no way to figure things out and to recognize reality
she has no one on her side to help her realize
that crimes are committed against her
there is no one to stop or educate her parents

the unconscious language of hatred and violence is forced deeply
into every cell of her body—before she can verbally communicate
the language of violence is passed on to her
and the energies of violence, hatred and evil are born
and brought into our world

the language of violence is a crime against humanity
but it is universally accepted as great wisdom
—taught and practiced all over the world—while we turn away
from the screams of the victims—mankind's children

23
a twisted concept of revenge

dreams of justice

the child was a terrified prisoner
imprisoned and tortured in a dark jail
that was filled with rules and regulations
orders and commands—punishments and beatings
where no light ever entered

life in the dungeon was about submission and obedience
actions and thoughts of revenge filled it—without anyone
ever acknowledging or naming them appropriately
cruel, evil actions by tyrannical parents
came along with sweeping declarations of the child's
—and only the child's—guilt and evilness

the hatred and despair sparked by the madness around her
prompted the child to dream of having power and getting even
of finding justice
of murdering those tyrants—but those dreams terrified her
and pushed her into irresolvable conflicts that eroded her sanity

she longed to love her parents and to be loved by them
she needed to see them as good and to be proud of them
—also—where would she go and how would she survive
without her parents?

any thoughts of revenge she discarded
because she wanted to be a good person
free of hatred—full of love and forgiveness

her dreams of justice remained unfulfilled

mask of discipline

the emotional and physical violence of my parents
was disguised as discipline
the child could not think of it as vengeance—passed on
from generation to generation
vindictiveness—silenced in childhood—that was finally allowed
to erupt toward a powerless target

the parent-child relationship is the only one
where inhuman behavior is allowed to continue
because we don't label it correctly

endless is the arsenal of degrading, cruel punishments
children are beaten with torture instruments like
        dress hangers, whips, belts, paddles
children are banned and isolated with barbaric inhumanity
        in rooms, closets or basements
children can be humiliated, cast out, contemptuously derided

my hands were put in gloves—my arms in braces
so that I could not suck my thumbs
my mouth—washed with soap for lying
but never was there any attempt to try to understand
why I sucked my thumb—I needed hugs and comfort
why I lied—the truth was not welcome and could not be told

buried hatred, disguised as discipline, maybe passed on
but speaking up against it and labeling parents' actions correctly
as hateful, dangerous, irresponsible and evil
is condemned as revengeful and unforgiving

the child's tortured Via Dolorosa as a victim of her parents' cruelty
is tolerated—even encouraged—by the world around
torture—inflicted in the name of "discipline" or "education"

nobody cared about a child's feelings and needs—her screams
were extinguished with pedagogical and moral clichés

how despised it is to mention the ordeal of childhood
judged as victim mentality
the child's suffering is forced deeper into silence

parental irresponsibility is not only excused
but even turned into the child's responsibility to forgive and forget

it is this abused child
who finds herself hopelessly condemned and cornered
always at the losing end
while her parents' cruelty is justified and excused

two standards create an insufferable, insane hypocrisy
where the weak are—even physically—tortured
for what is judged as their mistake and badness
while the strong and powerful are not held accountable

we need to listen and learn
we must change our view of the inhumanity and cruelty
masked for centuries as education and discipline

instead of extinguishing our children's screams
we need to teach parents the discipline
of love and mercy
of listening to their children
        with an open, compassionate mind
                with a loving soul
                        with a caring, devoted heart
and of answering and guiding them
truthfully
openly
and honestly

sunday school

I survived my childhood through a complete state of forgiveness
I was blamed—and blamed myself
for the abuse and any problem that occurred

as a young child in Sunday school
surrounded by the impressive church building
filled with reverence and grandiose solemnity
I felt small, unimportant, invisible, deeply intimidated

religious commands, reprimands, expectations were passed out
and became a scary brew of passed-on morality
that demanded "be good"—which meant above all
not to speak up
but to always be forgiving
and to silence
my pain and protest when I was wronged and hurt

church morality reinforced what I experienced at home
this powerful moralistic brew demanded a forgiving attitude
of the dependent, the defenseless and the powerless
while it declared the powerful infallible

to be a good person meant I should not utter my truth
should not be angry or protest
never contradict or ask the "wrong" questions

I did not even dare to think that my mother
was a frightening example of a non-forgiving person

my parents' beliefs and what I learned in Sunday school
imprinted me with constant messages to overlook abuse
to forgive perpetrators who commit abuse
and to ignore and invalidate their crimes as benefactions

this strange morality gave no permission to say *no*
to stand up for myself and speak up to abusive people
to stop their cruel actions

programmed to be a victim, I believed
that no matter what happened to me—I deserved it
should endure it without protest and forgive it with an open heart
—but never ask to be treated with humanity and respect

thus I learned to accept cruelty as immutable reality

I was sold a concept of "love" that gave powerful parents the right
to hold grudges, to commit any kind of arbitrary cruelty
be unforgiving and communicate verbally or physically their anger
it endorsed punitive actions that spoke of hatred and revenge

parents were not responsible for their actions
or for the unhappiness, pain, fear or confusion they caused
it was the child who was blamed
expected to endure, obey and be silent

the morality at home and in Sunday school reinforced
submission to every parental whim
forced the child's screams and outrage
—forbidden as revengeful—
deeper and deeper into silence

it did not encourage me to express to anyone what I saw and felt
it did not empower me to articulate what I realized and thought
it did not allow me to voice how terrified and lonely I was
it forbade me to share with anyone how I suffered in agony

the child was trained
that only forgiving one's enemy brought peace
—but the one person in this world whom she
experienced as her enemy
was her own mother

a new journey

the life I am seeking lies somewhere before me
the life I am rejecting now lies in my past
I am leaving behind senseless perceptions that have only
served to continue my suffering and misery
no longer will I sacrifice my truth to satisfy others

I suppressed the knowledge of pain my parents caused me
to spare them my reality—now I have reached the other side
where revenge and evil are committed by the powerful who hurt
powerless children—but not by those who speak up
against it—and demand to put an end to it

I have arrived at a new perspective
where obedient silence is not a virtue anymore
where life—above all the life of vulnerable children—
may not be hurt or destroyed through the abuse of power

life is created by meaningful action and loving support
in relationships that do not wish to inflict cruel pain
but accompany others with understanding and respect
and want them to grow and be themselves

life wants me to live in such a way
        that suffering and being injured
        acceptance and forgiveness of needless pain
        and sacrificing my truth and true Self
are no more its essence or at its core

life has been given to me as my responsibility
to protect my physical and emotional well-being and that of others

in my past it was judged as selfish if I took care of myself lovingly
today I know that I practice self-love when I am kind with my Self

24
farewells

leaving the fjord

I have left Chicago, my beloved home for six years
and my therapist, too—my harbor for eighteen months
I have returned to Germany

in the city where I was born and raised
I live again only minutes away from my parents

confronted by hostility I feel I am lost in a desert
without warmth, friendship and love

one day I play the piano for someone else who tells me
you play with such feeling
you have something very unique inside

that night I dream
>that I am safe at the end of a fjord on a boat with my father
>suddenly someone takes over the rudder
>and steers the ship with powerful security out of the fjord
>into the open sea
>my father objects and protests—*this is too dangerous*—*stop it*
>but the boat leaves the fjord
>
>then I find myself in a stormy, stirred-up sea
>drifting alone and lost in threatening waves
>near me I also see a child
>drifting further and further away from me
>our lives are in mortal danger
>a rubber boat comes—men want to get me out of the water
>I answer—*I will not come unless you save the child first*
>they save the child first—and then me

I wake up deeply moved

synagogue

I enter a room where I have never been in my life—a synagogue
my old, learned view of life, shaped by Christian religion
portrayed this place as dead, overcome, hostile
even dangerous and evil—without life
full of narrowing laws and arrogant self-righteousness

it takes courage to enter a synagogue
my son is invited to a Bar Mitzvah
I ask if I can attend the service—I am thirty-four years old

I am so afraid to enter a synagogue
—what a taboo where I come from—this house of God
        this religion, these human beings—
the religion I was taught portrayed this place as damned by God
the work of the devil—where a curse was cast
and a horrible spell created evil

I am in a room where I have never been
it is the modern, dramatic building of a liberal congregation
the service begins—the singing of the cantor moves my heart
the words of the prayer book move my soul
they hold so much truth for me—I start to cry

I believed that this was a dangerous place
without life—without wisdom—petrified in laws
but the lies I was taught by my religion and my origins
are unmasked in this place—this place is not dead
it is full of music and life, full of interesting, exciting thoughts
I hear truth
I feel at home, at one with the human beings who surround me
at one with Jews in their synagogue

the central thoughts of this service focus on
supporting conscious, responsible actions and treasuring life
no word about a last judgment, guilt, redemption through faith

I have never felt at home anywhere or with anyone in my life
here, I feel at home, listening to the values and ideas expressed
I cry through the whole service

I think about my country, Germany, where I did not know Jews
where are the synagogues? where is this form of life?
where are tolerance, soul, color
nobility of spirit and celebration of life?

the truth I have to realize takes my breath away
where I come from a unique way of life
was despised, destroyed, exterminated
where I come from this life and this culture
were expelled, banned, extinguished, murdered

I think about the religion I was taught
which indoctrinated me with blind faith and dangerous hatred
with fear of hell and a last judgment
today my path has turned further and deeper away from it
today I have left its confinements behind
today I have entered life—God's home

as I learn more about Christianity's contribution to anti-semitism
I am appalled
upon my return to Germany I leave the religion I was raised in

out of the fog

written in Germany, 1991

after I have left my first marriage I dream
  that I have been driving in the fog

   when the fog lifts
   I realize that I am on a narrow mountain road
   a steep abyss drops off to one side
   no railing to protect the cars from falling down

   I cannot turn the car around
   so I drive backwards
   carefully
   frightened
   wondering how I drove along that street—in the fog
   so close to the abyss
   amazed that I did not fall into that depth—to die

   I make it back to the main street
   now I can turn my car around
   to drive forward again

   I enter the main street
   and join the flow of traffic

   I am reunited with life

hopeless hope

after my first husband and I separate
we still see each other and spend time together
I hope that our marriage can be saved
he is polite and friendly—but remains distant

then one day I dream
> that I am sitting at home at my table
> with my husband sitting next to me on the side of the table
> we talk and I tell him—*I have given you three chances*
> *the first when I asked you to do therapy with me*
> *the second when I returned with you to Germany*
> *now I am giving you a third chance*
> *if you don't take this one there will be no other one*

in the following weeks I am flooded with anxiety every time
I think about this dream—until I write about it and realize
that the child would not have survived her childhood
without the hope that one day she could win her parents' love

but I, the adult woman, must admit to myself that with this man
my dreams of love cannot come true
the child's hopeless hope ties me to a man I also cannot reach
and makes me put my life on hold—while I suffer

as I free myself from the child's illusionary hope
I bring true hope into my life—the hope that I can escape
agony and unhappiness
that I can make my life happier
and go out to find the love I long for

the mountain
or—changing perspective

written in Chicago, January 2001

I am looking at a mountain—it reminds me of my mother
for most of my life I have looked at my mother
as if I was cursed to remain at the bottom of a mountain
with a confined, limited perspective

from the bottom the mountain is domineering
blocking out the view of the world and life around me

getting to know my Self has become like climbing a mountain

from the bottom I look up
I look at my mother with compassion
I look at her in the way she wants me to
I look at her as if I were her therapist

at the bottom of the mountain
I feel and have always felt forced to forgive my mother
to pity her
to ignore how she was—and is—treating me
to numb and deaden the suffering she causes me
to deny my own pain—to ignore reality and the truth

at the top of the mountain I have a wider view
I can see further

I see my mother from a different perspective
as I experience for the first time compassion for myself

I have to recognize the truth
I see a woman who does not love me

who does not take joy in my being
who does not care about my existence
who has no interest in my life
who does not desire to get together with me
after she has not seen me for thirteen years

I have to see the truth—although I don't want to
       my mother does not love me
       my mother cannot love who I am
       because I am the living proof
       that life is about other things than those
       that she believes in, lives by and practices

I am crushed by the truth
I feel the ground crumble beneath my feet
and my existence threatened

the truth hurts—but liberates me
I have escaped her jail

freed from the gravest impediment that kept me from being alive
I become the bird and fly away from the mountain

from now on my own welfare matters
my needs count

I cannot be alive without love
just as air gives life to my body—love is the breath for my soul

my soul would die if I stayed near this mountain

now that I know and can bear the truth
I leave the mountain
I am free to be Barbara
to be my Self

who am I?

broken into different parts
who would be Barbara's leader?
the deadly fear of my mother ruled fiercely over my actions
desperate love made me cling to my father
the hurt pride of the child who was replaced five times
and pushed away further and further
teamed up with the sinister loner—deeply afraid of people
they did not trust love but avoided it as a dangerous illusion
although my loneliness thirsted for companionship and love

anger and hatred born from cruel injustice craved revenge
while the showpiece wanted to make her parents proud
my hatred of patriarchy's madness wanted to "show them"
survival fears that tormented me craved safety and predictability

within me lived the powerless nothing who felt unimportant
like a number—who believed her life did not matter
within me lived a paranoid skeptic, afraid to trust
within me lived the silenced coward who did not dare to speak up
within me cowered the blind one who closed her eyes firmly
who clung to illusions and idealized
within me sobbed the desperate one who wanted to give up

for the longest time I did not know—who am I?
broken off parts fought obsessively over who would have power
over me—each one believed it knew what is best for me
how I should live, how to protect me, how to make me safe
their beliefs and emotions were formed and remained stuck
in their traumatic experiences—they had nothing to do with me

as they change and let go
my inner turmoil is relieved
and the warring enemies inside—become my supportive friends

NO—my hidden guide through life

after the incest memory had resurfaced
a surprising force inside of me could emerge
and become conscious

early in my life this part felt a passionate **NO**
towards my mother's violence, temper and strictness
towards any form of cruelty and degradation
towards injustice and terror
after the incest—unbeknown to me—
this passionate **NO** became a **scream of NO**

as it threatened other parts of me that craved approval
I had to hide this **NO** from my Self for many years
but it shaped my life powerfully from the underground

this **NO** grew stronger and deeper when I learned
about the Holocaust and the crimes of Nazi Germany
this knowledge questioned profoundly everything
that my parents and ancestors lived and believed
—their values, their ways of life, their religion
           their national and class consciousness

this **NO** asked me to leave behind their beliefs
it desired to end the hypocrisy that had conducted their lives
their marriages and families
it demanded to overcome their arrogance

this scream of **NO** guided my life powerfully
—as a young mother it asked me to treat my children differently
and helped me face the disapproval it entailed
—in my thirties it took me into therapy
empowered me to pursue it
           —despite my first husband's criticism—

235

gave me the strength to stand up to his objections
face my mother's hostility, reproachfulness
        and incomprehensible lack of understanding
let me survive my family's painful silence and abandonment
        which banished me into exile

this **NO** enabled me to withdraw from painful relationships
leave my country and background
empowered me to find love where I was not supposed to look

this **NO** brought out my calling
encouraged me to break silences within and around me
it wants me to help shed light on
how evil and cowardly fear are being produced

for the longest time I had been too afraid
that I would hurt my mother with what I was writing
this **NO** guided me strongly away from her
and from those who don't want the truth to live

this **NO** knew that my life was not given to me
to continue the destructiveness of my background
and to serve parental beliefs—but to serve life

this **NO** knew that I am not here
to obey and follow parents whose lies and self-deception
ruled a silenced family
but to appreciate and honor my own life, voice and destiny

when at fifty I met and was united with my **NO**
I became empowered to embrace my self-expression
as the contribution I was meant to make to life

my **NO** believes in change
my **NO** fights for justice and humanity for children
my **NO** encourages me to write and publish this book

black figure

written in Chicago, 1985

after six years of tremendous changes I live in Germany again
while I visit Chicago the following summer I have a dream
>in my dream I travel twice to the same country
>the first time I carry a black figure on my back
>holding on to me with a tight, painful grip

>when I return for the second time
>the black figure has slipped off me and goes away

upon awakening I write the image and my feelings down:

black figure, your face destroyed and torn
your body tall and huge, your limbs are stiff and awkward

black figure, you were my companion for a long time
forever I was buried under your weight that burdened my walk
your grip around my chest squeezed my heart
and the pain would spread through my body
to leave it on endless trails of tears

your presence kept away good friends—joy of life and love

black figure, slowly you are walking away

as you leave you pull away your black dress which covered me
your dress is sinking down from my body
only its seam still touches me gently

black companion without face
I see you disappear in the distance—the sight makes me cry

free

written in Mexico, 2004

as I near the end of my work on this book
I have a dream about my father

    I see my father leaning against a wall
    his legs cannot carry him anymore
    he is about to break down

    I put my body under his body
    his lower chest rests on my shoulders
    he is very ill and vomits
    completely limp he is hanging across my back

    I don't know what to do with my father
    a sister and brother are in the house
    they talk to me and notice me
    neither hostile nor interested in my burden and my problem
    they don't help me

    someone else arrives to take care of my father
    he tells me—*just put him down*

    I see two beds
    one is for two people
    the other for one person only—this is where I put my father down
    I push him up so that he can lie better on the bed
    and I mention to my brothers and sisters
    that he is not heavy anymore
    they agree but remain distant and indifferent

25
bringing forgiveness to the child who was never forgiven

buried under a mountain of tar

buried under a mountain of tar—the child is invisible
so much blame, shame and hatred have been piled upon her
that you cannot see her anymore
you don't even know that she is there
completely isolated from contact with any living being
she is totally alone
surrounded by all that black tar stuff that tells her
you are not a lovable person—you are wrong

never-ending blame and guilt—the incest—the car accident
produced more and more tar
no way could she ever get out from under all that black tar

trapped where there is no light she feels painfully
the weight and heat of the mountain of tar that surrounds her
she torments herself always with the same questions
what am I doing that is so wrong? why am I being criticized?
what must I do to make everyone around me happy?
the one question she can never dare to ask herself is
—what will make me happy?

destructive madness and inhuman nonsense were piled upon her
what a crime to heap all this on a vulnerable child
who cannot fight back or see through what is going on
much less walk away from it

to the child trapped in this dark place I bring a light
I reach out to the terrified child who believed false accusations
I gently hold her and calm her fears
I ask her if she will walk with me and leave behind
all the expectations, the guilt and the blame
that have been burdening her spirit
she takes my hand and I lead her on the path to freedom

241

the land of unforgiveness

every step of the alive child was treated like a crime
perceived by her parents as a mistake—or even a sin
innocent steps brought terror and disaster instead of loving help
timid, insecure steps into life evoked catastrophic judgments
justified by gruesome interpretations and accusations
endless was the arsenal to degrade and hurt the child

forgiveness was preached—but childhood was
the land of unforgiveness—where forgiveness was not practiced
the myths of education and discipline permitted
every unforgiving attitude and action imaginable under the sun
and used the child as a defenseless, powerless victim

why are those without power reprimanded and punished
while those with power must be unconditionally forgiven?
why was the child never forgiven—but taught to always forgive?

children, so completely reliant on others for their survival
must experience forgiveness
it is the vital nourishment for their humanity

show me, mother, the spirit of forgiveness
don't be merciless and brutally strict—ban physical punishment
stop inflicting pain on me through your words and actions
with what you believe and think about me—with how you see me
too many wounds and hurt places inside me stem from it
they render me powerless

you did not practice forgiveness with your child
unforgiveness ruled your kingdom
it kept my soul your captive and my Self your slave
until I forgave myself for choosing a different way of life
—you never forgave me for leaving your world of unforgiveness

we shed pain and hatred

I know—parents have a past, often were abused, too—
but that does not give them the right to take it out on me

the child inside needs to know that she can communicate
her pain and outrage to me—and trust that I will not silence her
because when she remembers and difficult memories come up
she needs to share them and be heard

on the waves of her pain and mourning I receive and accept
her anger and hatred for the crimes committed against her
that no one named crimes or abuse but "for her own good"

when she has shared her feelings and experiences with me
her anger and hatred pass
her pain subsides and she can enjoy life again

never ever will I ask of her not to communicate feelings
that never could live and never were heard before

she has my unconditional permission to experience
and express all her feelings to me
if I told her to forgive—she would not dare to speak up

I listen—to liberate her from the horrors of her past
piece by piece we shed the pain and hatred of the past

I forgive her for feeling hurt, outraged and hateful
I listen to her and let her unload those long-buried feelings
I don't tell her to stop because I have had enough
I don't ask of her that she must "let go"—instead
I am there for her—she can count on me

I want to be the parent she never had

forgiveness—what does it mean?

"I will never forgive you for abandoning me
when I needed you the most"
      my mother's comment to me in 1984

for years I faced an unforgiving mother
and suffered from her hostility and resentment
I was never forgiven for needing and entering therapy
for changing and becoming my Self
for no longer being the perfect eldest daughter

but the demand for forgiveness is always placed upon me—why?
what does forgiveness mean?
my mother's hostility hurts me when I am with her
I have most painfully felt
her reproachful rejection of me and my life's journey
of my values and goals, of my thoughts and feelings

why is the moral burden to forgive placed upon me?
why must I suffer from her unwillingness to change
when I can find inner peace without her?
what does the repeated demand for forgiveness truly mean?

isn't it the same thing that was asked of me as a child?
to turn off my feeling—the sacred gift of life—
every time I am with my mother, facing her resentment
her hostility and anger toward me?

doesn't it mean that I should pretend that all is well
become a hypocrite in her presence
that I should ignore my feelings and the pain she causes me
that I must murder my truth and my soul—to please her
to continue what I did to survive as a child?

for her? to serve her to be a forgiving girl? a "good girl"? a liar?

no—my soul screams—**no**—**no more**—I cannot do this anymore
I die if I have to lie to get love
after having worked so hard to resurrect my feelings and needs
I will honor them
I will appreciate and serve life within me
by not discarding and abandoning my feelings
and thus my Self ever again

how can I sacrifice my soul, my integrity and self-protection
ignore my own well-being and love for my Self all over again
for her
she who has given me life demanded
that I extinguish life within me, give up my vitality for her
the vitality I fought so hard to rescue and resurrect

from now on I refuse to suffer needless pain
and resentment may no longer gnaw away at me
I cannot be part of a hopeless relationship anymore

as I have allowed forgiveness to enter my life
I have forgiven—myself
for trying so long and so hard—completely in vain—
to reach my mother, to enable our relationship
and to fill it with truth, honesty and love

I have brought into my life the permission
to protect and liberate my Self from incessant pain
so that my soul can heal and soar

forgiveness means—the screams can be voiced
pain and outrage can leave body, mind and soul
the truth is shared, accepted and becomes consciously known
I am at peace—accepting that I am without mother

forgiveness flows where honesty and truth can live
if they can't—forgiveness becomes nothing
but a deceptive device to deny reality, to conceal the truth
and life is forced into a lie

the land of forgiveness

in the land of forgiveness every child is regarded
as a blessing of the divine
whom we must meet with reverence and the deepest respect
and unconditional forgiveness
as if the child Jesus had entered our lives
whose parents believed he was the child of God

in the land of forgiveness every child is regarded
as an angel from the universe of love
who has come to visit us so that we may become
as loving and forgiving as we possibly can be

in the land of forgiveness every child is regarded
as a precious gift of life—like a most treasured orchid—
that can only grow and blossom with the utmost care
of devoted and unconditional love

in the land of forgiveness every child carries inside
the holy essence of life
parents and society have the task to bring it out and let it shine
to unfold the creativity, the uniqueness, the divinity
entailed in this precious essence
that may never be attacked or injured

in the land of forgiveness every child is regarded
as a sacred messenger of the divine
who may never be spoken to or treated harshly or cruelly
never be tortured with acts of inhuman, brutal violence
who may never be ridiculed, derided, humiliated, degraded
because it would hurt the divine essence inside
make it withdraw—and go away

26
walking together into life

my feelings are like a universe
written in 1988

my feelings are like a universe
a wide, alive, endless
world
within me

they fill my whole body from top to toe
everywhere
all the way into my fingertips

they make me feel alive
they make me feel that I exist

my feelings turn my inside into an enchanted space
into a magnificent cathedral of vitality
embracing and holding life

through my feelings and thoughts I experience life within me
they create
me
Barbara
my uniqueness

when I feel—I am my Self

until now I only knew the medicated smile of a mask
who fulfilled expectations pleasantly
as fear, guilt, confusion ruled her inner world

but now
feelings and thoughts become wishes and dreams—even goals
I want to make them come true

the child—coming into my arms

one more time—for the very last time
I have let the empress arise over her child
threateningly she throws condemnations against her child
as she seeks to shatter the truth and the child's self-confidence

on the battlefield of vengeance I have found the child
through therapy, patience, perseverance and my love
I have come to rescue her
I take her in my arms and carry her away to safety and freedom
far away from the battlefield and the old order of things
which is not mine—I now clearly recognize the battlefield
for its destructiveness

after a long struggle where the battlefield caught, enveloped her
again and again—telling her how bad she was
        if she did not follow those old rules and beliefs—
she is now able to trust me—to come along into a new life
the child and I leave behind values and people
who cause us, and others, harm and pain

as I enter the freedom of authenticity and self-expression
I leave behind self-denial and the war against the true Self
I build a life where integrity, seeking the truth, breaking silences
are embraced as values

incapable of grasping yet that she is safe, free and forgiven
—truly leaving that dark and destructive place—
the child cries—she can hardly believe that her ordeal is over
that her sorrow and suffering are acknowledged
that her tears are allowed to flow

she hugs me and I hold her while I carry her away
to other people and to a different life journey we make together

walking together into life

frightened and terrified—the child in my arms
I comfort her—I hold her—I make her feel safe

behind her—terrified
generations of mothers and fathers scream—*don't go*
don't trust yourself—never trust your true Self

but I dare to step into the unknown
I am holding the child's hand now
she wants to walk by my side

still full of fear—listening to those voices—
she makes timidly her very first steps into life

I gently talk to her and encourage her to trust me
to trust that I will care for her—that we will be all right
that life is not like the nightmares of her past
to trust that we don't need a lifeline anymore
clinging to and holding onto others who tell us
how we should be, what to do and what to believe
who want to judge and define us

with warmth and love I support her to take her first steps
these are revolutionary steps
away—from the destructive, violent battlefield
out—of unbearable horror
out—of the dungeon filled with unimaginable fear and terror

what was familiar territory seemed until now safer
than the world outside—than reality and life
safer—than the truth—than to trust my true Self

I am holding her hand—she is holding my hand

she is beginning to trust me
and to walk with me

tears are streaming from our eyes, down our cheeks
tears of sorrow, mourning the past
tears of joy, welcoming life
we cry and laugh together—full of fear and joy

we celebrate this incredible moment
we marvel how it ever happened—how it ever was possible
that we found each other and can be together

that we could escape the dungeon and be free
to walk together, hand in hand, into life

Thank you!

This book is built on the support of wonderful human beings:
I am grateful to my therapists Allen Siegel,
Gina Demos, Richard Schwartz, and Melody Allen,
who helped me face my past.

I am grateful to Alice Miller, whose courageous books
inspired me to break the power of my past and claim my life.

I am grateful for precious friendships: Heide, Lucy, Alice,
Ortrun, Dieter, Jerry, Eva and Eva, Stephanie, Marina, Jutta,
Reni, Guilly, Marlys, MaryCarmen, and my cousin Regina.

I am grateful for the encouragement and great help
of my editors Amy, Sareda and Earl,
and of the writers' group in San Miguel with
Marge, Sareda, Gabriella, Helen, Dorothy, and Ken.

I am grateful to Silvia,
who provided the gift of time for writing and of time for myself.

I am grateful to my youngest brother Andreas,
whose support creates a miraculous haven for the "lost daughter."

I am grateful for the love of my children, Max and Sebastian,
and of my daughter-in-law, Ute. They have granted me
generous support for my rather unusual life journey.

I am grateful to my granddaughters, Hannah and Marlene,
for all the joy they bring into my life.

I am grateful to my step-children Sarah, Rose, and David,
and my most loveable step-grandson Preston
for the love we have shared.

I am grateful to Earl, whose love carried me into life.
His support helped me accomplish my journey and this book.

Barbara Rogers was born in 1950 in Germany.
She lives in the United States and Mexico.
She is active as a piano teacher, chamber musician,
photographer, painter, and writer.

Her essay "Facing a Wall of Silence"
is published in *Second Generation Voices*,
edited by Naomi and Alan Berger,
published in 2001 by Syracuse University Press.

Printed in the United Kingdom
by Lightning Source UK Ltd.
107866UKS00001B/77